How to
Stop Your Papers from Killing You (and me)

Notes for a Quiet Revolution

Also by Keith Harrison

Poetry

Points in a Journey
Songs from the Drifting House
The Basho Poems
A Burning of Applewood (New & Selected Poems)
Words Against War
The Complete Basho Poems
Changes: New & Collected Poems, 1962–2002

Selected readings from these books can be heard at keithharrison.org

Translations

Sir Gawain and the Green Knight (Oxford World's Classics)
At the Wedding of Peleus & Thetis: Catullus #64 (with Linda Clader)

Radio Drama

The Water Man
Sir Gawain and the Green Knight

Theater

The Papers of Lady Ann Vaughn
Sir Gawain and the Green Knight

Forthcoming

Once Upon a River: Selected Essays

How to Stop Your Papers from Killing You (and me)

Notes for a Quiet Revolution

KEITH HARRISON

Copyright © 2012 by Keith Harrison (keithharrison.org)

All rights reserved under International and Pan-American Copyright Conventions. For permission to reprint material in this text (except as allowed by fair use) contact Black Willow Press.

ISBN 978-0-939394-16-6

Published in the United States by Black Willow Press.

www.blackwillowpress.com

Book design by Mark F. Heiman

for Judy Daniel

Contents

FOR STUDENTS: A Preliminary Word	1
A Note for My Colleagues	2
PART I: LANCE AND THE SACRED COWS	3
ONE: Lance Surprises Himself	5
TWO: Through an Hourglass, Darkly	8
THREE: How to be a Person in Your Writing	15
FOUR: What Lance Discovered	20
First Interlude: The Hidden Power of Free-Writing	27
PART II: ILIAD or A Model for All Seasons	32
FIVE: The Structure of ILIAD	35
SIX: A Note on Writing in the Sciences	48
PART III: FIVE ALTERNATIVE FORMS	53
SEVEN: The False Thesis	55
EIGHT: Dialogues and Dialectics	60
NINE: Approaching Sideways	65
TEN: Prismatic Composition	69
ELEVEN: Mixed Forms	75
PART IV: TWO KEYS TO EFFECTIVE NARRATION	77
TWELVE: Quotations as Characters	79
THIRTEEN: Mastering Transitions	83
Second Interlude: The Uses of Précis-Writing	89
PART V: FINE-TUNING: WHERE THE ANGELS LIVE	99
FOURTEEN: Pointers for Editing	101
FIFTEEN: Honing Your Conclusion, Finding a Title	106
SIXTEEN: Epilogue	111

FOR STUDENTS:
A Preliminary Word

For many years I've worked on the firm conviction that most students can write much better than they usually do and that the chief things that inhibit fresh and authentic writing are fixed conceptions about what an essay is. My aim in this book is to encourage you to explore alternative forms of composition that will allow you to break away from restrictive habits and write more naturally. As you become more fully engaged with your subject and the individual shaping that each essay requires you will begin to write prose that's more interesting for your readers, and yourself. That will, in turn, give you more confidence.

If you give the method outlined here a sustained trial I'm convinced you will experience a sense of liberation. Although the main focus of this book is on the writing of academic essays, the skills you develop as you try this new approach will be useful not only in college but in all your later writing, whatever form it might take.

The approach in this book probably differs rather sharply from the one you're used to and it may cause you some initial discomfort. Some of that discomfort may come from wondering how it will be greeted by your teachers. Let me deal with that directly. If you're convinced that this new method might work for you it would be sensible to consult with your teacher before you try any of the alternatives I'm proposing. You may be advised not to depart from your usual practice. You should take that advice seriously. However, if you don't have the chance to try out the more ambitious strategies in this book you may still find some of the ideas on such matters as the use of the first person, free-writing, quotations, transitions and précis-writing of some help.

*

All the examples of student writing, as well as many of the other quoted passages in this book, are inventions. In a few places I've quoted from published sources. In devising the excerpts from students' essays I've tried to make all the examples relevant to the kind of problems students commonly encounter in their writing.

For information about formatting, bibliographies, footnotes, and all the professional requirements of academic essays there are a number of excellent handbooks available, so I've not dealt with those matters in this book. Your teachers have probably recommended, or will recommend appropriate texts to guide you with any technical or scholarly questions you might have in your essay-writing. If not, I would suggest you keep a copy of the MLA Style Sheet close to hand. It's very useful for most purposes.

A Note for My Colleagues

Although this text is primarily intended for students who are having difficulty with their writing, and for those who would like to explore new possibilities, I hope it will also be useful for teachers at all levels of essay-writing. It's one person's answer to problems encountered in using traditional methods over many years, and its assumptions might seem somewhat radical, even though they're based on ideas about writing that go back to Plato. If you're reluctant to go along with its overall approach you may still find sections of the book of practical help—particularly those on free-writing, "voice," précis-writing, the use of quotations and the art of transitions. My chief aim is to help students gain a sense of purpose and pleasure in their writing. If this book serves, even in a small way, to achieve that double aim I'll consider myself more than adequately rewarded.

PART I
LANCE AND THE SACRED COWS

ONE:
Lance Surprises Himself

Lance Judkins sits down at his computer with a slight sense of desperation. He has to get this thing done. He begins typing:

> In the cultural history of Japan, works of art have always played an important role, not just in houses and museums but also in public places. In this essay I will discuss one form of public art in Japan — the temple-garden. These gardens can be found throughout Japan. They are nothing at all like American gardens. They are also very important to the Japanese because they reveal a great deal about Japanese culture and thought. Many historians have written about the particular part that temple-gardens play in Japanese life...

Suddenly, he stops and lets his hands fall from the keyboard. He stares disconsolately out the window. Once again he has the old sinking feeling about his own writing. There's no voice in it and it all sounds formal and willed. He can't understand why everything he writes comes out so deadly dull.

Lance's assignment is to write a five-page paper for his course on Asian Religions and Culture (Religion 277). His task is to compare Japanese thought as it's embodied in a particular institution with what we think of as typically western modes of thought. He's chosen the topic of temple-gardens because he's been interested in Japanese art and culture for a number of years and has recently returned from a semester in Kyoto, during which time his understanding of things Japanese, including temple-gardens, has deepened considerably.

Right now he's recovering from a week of debilitating flu and the deadline's fast approaching. He has to be efficient.

He glances at the pile of "information" on his desk. He knows that very soon after this blah opening he'll have to state his thesis, and he doesn't want to do that because, if this first paragraph is half-dead, stating his thesis immediately will kill his paper outright. What was, potentially, a very interesting topic is rapidly turning into a formal exercise. He can't get away from the nagging question in his head: *How can I turn all this into something coherent —and interesting to read?* It's at this point where many students lose interest in what they are writing.

Lance leans back in his chair and looks up at the ceiling and thinks back on his time in Japan. A vivid memory floats into his mind of a sunlit day when, on a whim, he took a detour down a side street he'd not explored before. *That was a typical temple-garden,* he says to himself, *and I know it well. Why not start there?*

He turns back to the keyboard, hits DELETE and begins afresh:

> A mile east from the center of Kyoto, in a modest little side-street, there's an opening in a stone wall. If you walk by it quickly it will hardly catch your attention. But if you stop and peer in you'll notice something unusual. Behind the narrow opening you there's a large flat expanse of raked gravel from which three rocks stand out like treeless mountains on the model of a desert landscape. The rocks are black and smooth and don't seem to form part of an obvious pattern. As you look beyond the rocks you see there's a very old building whose beams are worn and weathered. There are also some old men, who appear to be monks, sitting quietly in the courtyard.
>
> My curiosity was aroused a great deal by what I saw. Why such a dry, formal garden, and what was the relation between the garden and the monastery?

Lance reads over what he's written and sits back feeling quite pleased. Although he's not totally conscious of the nature of the sharp change he's made he senses that it's really significant. He's right. Lance has discovered a special kind of transformation which, from that moment on, is going to affect everything he writes.

TWO:
Through an Hourglass, Darkly

Very few of the thousands of student writers I've been lucky enough to teach so far have suffered from verbal incompetence. Yet only a handful of their essays have held my attention to the end. It took me years to understand the discrepancy between their obvious verbal ability and the way they expressed their ideas on the page. It baffled me so much that, in my darker moments, I use to wonder if we'd made a pact to hurt each other. Hence the title of this book.

One morning on my way into class I had to step over one of my students who had fallen asleep across the threshold. When I leaned down and asked if he was okay, he muttered something about "up all night doing your paper." I knew right then that something had to be done. The primary thought that impelled me from that moment was this: if you're struggling very hard and still writing below your potential there's nearly always a simple reason for it. *It's not your fault. You've been trained over a period of many years to adopt a method of writing which has inhibited your capacity for genuine thought.* Chances are that you were required to learn the "correct" approach in high school and, because you've been told it's essential, especially at college, you're still using it. Yet even if you've mastered the method it hardly ever brings you a sense of satisfaction. If that's where you are right now, we're all losers: you, me, and your essays.

There's a way to change all this.

What I'm offering you is an invitation to join me in conducting what William Blake called a mental war—in this case a war against some sacred cows which have caused us all a lot of unnecessary trouble. The first, though not the only one, is the mode of writing which is called variously the five-paragraph or hourglass method. It's taught so widely it seems to many students and teachers part of the natural order. From now on I'll call it the hourglass model. So that we can be sure we're talking about the same thing let's rehearse its basic shape:

> An introduction, in which
> you state your thesis and
> foreshadow your three supporting
> proofs or arguments.
> First proof
> or argument;
> second proof
> or argument;
> third proof
> or argument.
> A conclusion which restates the
> thesis and summarizes your three
> supporting proofs or arguments.

The directives for this model can be put like this:
—Always state your thesis/conclusion very near the beginning;
—Your essay, as a whole, must make a clear well-supported *assertion*;
—You must always have three "proofs" for your main assertion;
—In case your reader is mentally asleep you must state your thesis at the beginning as well as the end of your paper.

Because this little quartet of imperatives nearly always leads to poor writing we have to challenge them. Let's take them in turn.

—When you state your thesis early in your essay you will spend a good deal of time fighting against anticlimax. Every writer knows that, yet most students cling to this rule tenaciously, even though it will require enormous effort to keep a half-dead creature half-alive. The effort is nearly always futile.

—Most of us learn nearly all we know by asking questions and arriving at partial answers. Then we ask more questions and get more partial answers. This process goes on until we die. Some questions, such as the "true" meaning of a poem by Wallace Stevens, or the nature of magnetism, or whether the NAFTA treaty helps the American economy—and hundreds of others—don't have, and may never have, final answers. The hourglass model doesn't allow us to raise questions about them. It requires us, in all instances, to make a firm, provable assertion in the form of a thesis. In doing that, it often goes against the way we actually think and learn.

—I've never met anyone who can explain why the major argument in an essay must have three parts. Perhaps it has something to do with the doctrine of the Trinity. I don't know. Whatever the reason, it won't hold up to scrutiny. Some major ideas come in many parts, some—such as Einstein's $E=MC^2$—in only one. To imagine that the number three is somehow holy is pure superstition.

—Finally, to condescend to your audience by repeating what you said in the first paragraph is to show the same kind of distrust that your instructors show toward you when they force you into the hourglass mold. The underlying rationale is: *you are not very capable, nor are your readers. This is a simple and rational scheme. Keep away from the fancy stuff, and get on with it!*

That last rationale skirts a host of problems. The hourglass model might look simple but it's very difficult to work with, and it's certainly not a rational scheme; it only seems so. So we can't follow the directive "get on with it!" because "it" is not a static thing. Each essay presents a different set of challenges.

The usual reason the educational establishment gives for insisting on the hourglass model runs this way: *Students' minds are so disorganized that they need a clear structure even to begin writing coherently. This structure is the best available and it suits all occasions.* This is an extraordinarily muddle-headed kind of reasoning. Most of the serious-minded students I've known don't think or write out of total incoherence. True, their thoughts don't come out fully formed, but that applies to all of us. We have to work to make our writing clear to ourselves, and to our audience. The hourglass model, far from assisting in this process, provides only the appearance of order and logic. Our ideas come to us in a great variety of shapes and bundles. When we try to cram them into a uniform package we destroy the possibility of authentic thinking and questioning before we begin to write.

The hourglass model is therefore *not* a universally useful matrix. On the contrary, in writing that requires sustained and authentic exploration it has little place.

There's another, somewhat hidden reason for the prevalence of this model in our schools and colleges, which goes like this: *when all students write their papers in this way it's much easier for their instructors to grade them.* The premise on which that statement rests is truly disturbing. If the level playing-field theory is chiefly for the convenience of teachers we should, for very obvious reasons, scrap it. Education is not primarily for the benefit of teachers.

When we stand back, what we see is this: at about the same time as the idea of universal education took root in the West, some well-meaning but highly unimaginative educators on both sides of the Atlantic decided it was necessary for students to write *all* their essays in a five-paragraph grid. Because these gentleman wore starch collars and were very serious and influential, the idea stuck. It's persisted to the present because teachers still find it convenient. The elephant in the room is this: both teachers and students also find it mind-numbingly tedious. There are much more productive possibilities close to hand.

The accepted model of writing has an even deeper rationale which is rarely acknowledged. Its aim is to maintain the status quo. It does that by privileging a kind of "thinking" which is bland, empty and safe. Its formal requirements stop the writer (in this case, you) from asking difficult questions or arguing for a view that challenges accepted wisdom. To illustrate, here's the highly condensed outline of an actual paper I once received on *Hamlet as Tragic Hero*:

Introduction/Thesis

Some people have claimed that Hamlet wasn't a tragic hero but I wish to show that this is not true because he showed three of the traits that we expect to find in a tragic hero: courage, nobility, clarity of purpose.

Body of the Essay

Three paragraphs, one on each of the above traits, with examples from the text of the play.

Conclusion/ Repetition of Thesis

It will be clear, then, that despite the numerous critiques made against Hamlet's status as a tragic hero, his manifestation of these heroic characteristics certainly qualifies him for inclusion in the company of tragic heroes.

We've all read, and most of us have written, essays like this at some stage. The quality of thought involved hardly needs comment. It's almost as if the author is determined *not* to think. Where does his unspoken definition of a tragic hero come from? Answer: nowhere. The words "tragic hero" in this essay will mean what the author wants them to mean. And why these three "proofs?" Well, it doesn't really matter. Almost any three will do. The fact is, nothing matters in this essay except satisfying the formula and getting the monkey off your back.

I once showed this example, in completed form, to a writing class and they asked me how I would grade it. My answer was simple. This Hamlet paper, along with countless others in the same mold (pun intended), is not an essay in any real sense. It represents a totally barren kind of thinking and writing. It doesn't rise anywhere near the level of an F because that grade is reserved for a writer who tries something and fails. This writer hasn't tried anything. His training, such as it is, has prompted him to produce nothing but quintessential mickey-mouse.

One can hardly imagine a more deadening waste of time.

Another very common justification for the hourglass model is that students must learn it before they move on to more creative forms of writing. It doesn't take much reflection to see that this is nonsense. We don't teach a person to hit a tennis-ball by strapping her upper arm to her body and, when she can manage to hit the ball with this crippling disadvantage, unstrap her arm so she can swing more freely. We encourage her to hit naturally, if awkwardly, from the outset and, by practice, gradually learn to hit better. The same should apply to writing.

To borrow from Wallace Stevens' notion on the three imperatives of poetry, I would say that the three things you should learn to cultivate in your writing are naturalness, the "play" of the imagination, and pleasure. I've already mentioned naturalness. Let me just add that you achieve naturalness in your prose when it sounds as if it's coming from a human being. Lance's revised opening is a case in point.

The second and third imperatives need a further note. Experience tells me that less than fifty percent of college students experience any creative pleasure in the writing of their papers. Some of my colleagues put the figure much lower. Be that as it may, it seems inarguable that very few seem capable of what I would call an "authentic" paper when they use the traditional method. And even fewer are able to write an interesting one. These things are connected.

Some people maintain, very vigorously, that imagination and pleasure have no part in academic writing. If they mean that at present little emphasis is given to them, they are largely correct. But if they mean that there *should* be no place for these two things I believe they are utterly wrong. In fact it is this widespread belief that makes so much writing in academia so grindingly tedious. Surely even the most jaded among us would agree that the exploration of ideas on the page can be one of the most rewarding activities of the human mind. That activity cannot take place without the Imagination. I'm using that word in the Coleridgean sense, which implies the joy of finding hidden connections and the testing of fresh ideas. It goes without saying that writing an essay also involves hard work. What I want to insist on is that authentic and pleasurable exploration are also essential to all good writing, including the writing of academic papers. When you really understand that idea you will never let it go. That was the turning-point for Lance, and that's what this book is about.

THREE:
How to be a Person in Your Writing

Everyone's been told at some time never to use the first person when writing an essay. Some teachers, on encountering the first "I," refuse to read the rest of the paper until it, and all the others, are removed. Most aren't so severe, but there's still a widespread notion that to write in the first person is to dishonor some unspoken law of nature. This dogma has caused so much confusion that we need to sort it out. If we look at it in the kindest possible light we have to acknowledge that the original perpetrators of the rule were trying to discourage students from using an academic paper as the occasion for a private and directionless ramble. This embargo is born of distrust. Very few students in their academic work feel compelled to write that kind of essay anyway. In logic this kind argument is known as a straw man. In dread of that straw man, the original founders, helped by thousands of later disciples in schools everywhere, have succeeded in encouraging you to write in a way in which there's no sense of a living person.

Just as it's impossible to write a readable essay using the old structure it's also impossible to write one if you pretend to be someone else, or worse, to be nobody. When you do that, here's what you produce:

> Since the dawn of history mankind has found the need to devise a system of education. In the Western World this has taken many forms. Plato had very strong ideas on what he wanted the Greek system to be, and he has had many followers right up to the present time. He has also had his detractors. Since the founding of America a number of thinkers

have helped shape the ideas which are still part of our legacy, and one of those is Thomas Dewey...

The trouble with this kind of prose is that there's no one at home. Sometimes I lie awake at night and imagine thousands of paragraphs like this one pouring out of schools and campuses all over the world, adding more detritus to the huge and invisible City of Dead Words. The writer of that paragraph has added one more tiny offering to the rubble-heap. With so many interesting things to occupy our minds, why are so many intelligent people wasting so much time?

If you're suffering from an ingrained tendency to write as if you're not present, there's a simple stratagem to get beyond it: read your work aloud and ask yourself, "Does this sound like the voice of a person saying something important to him or her—or does it sound like the passage above?" If your prose doesn't pass the voice test there's something wrong, and you can do something about it. You need to find ways make your writing sound like the voice of a living person: yourself.

Technically, there are two acceptable ways of doing this. The first is to use an *implied* first person narrator without actually using the word "I":

> ...What Dickens tells us about Mr. Pickwick is so full of lively detail that, as in all good fiction, it has the immediacy of "felt life." Mr. Pickwick is palpably "there" for us. Perhaps it would be more accurate to say that Dickens writes *as if* Mr. Pickwick is there, both for him and us. Those little words are crucially important. "As if" is the defining mode of fiction. We, the readers, know that Mr. Pickwick is an invention, yet we willingly suspend our disbelief because we also know that the art of reading about him is to pretend, with the author, that he really does exist...

The second is to write *directly* in the first person, making sure your primary attention is on the subject you are discussing:

> ...Malmsby would reply that it may well be that the fact that Hitler was a house-painter is relatively insignificant, but there are thousands of other facts about Hitler and his period which we should not either omit or distort in the name of some overarching ideology... **From where I stand now**, it seems something important is being said by both these authors .

Both these passages are from the same essay and, taken together, they illustrate that the question of voice in your writing can't be reduced to the choice of "I" or "not I." That's a superficial, though very common, way of judging the "correctness" of your prose. These two passages also make it clear that whether or not you use the first person in your essay is a red herring. It ignores the real problem. That problem, which we all face, including professional writers, is this: How can I write both authentically and consequentially? I would claim that the writer of the above two paragraphs has achieved both these things, and her use of the direct first person in the second excerpt shouldn't be grounds for disqualifying the whole essay. That's to pick nits for no good reason. It's a question of where the emphasis lies, and in both these examples it lies firmly in the subject matter. The author's use of the word "I" in the second excerpt is a natural consequence of her thinking about the topic, not some kind of willful anarchy. Although she is not the central focus of her essay, the author is still an essential presence. Any grounds for suppressing the use of the first person in a case like this are based not on reasoned argument but on an unthinking mental reflex.

If you're still not convinced, here's another example:

> I stand at the window of a railway carriage which is traveling uniformly, and drop a stone on the embankment, without throwing it. Then, disregarding the influence of the air resistance, I see the stone descend in a straight line. A pedestrian who observes the misdeed from the footpath notices that the stone falls to earth in a parabolic curve. I now ask: Do the "positions" traversed by the stone lie "in reality" on a straight line or on a parabola?

The scientist who wrote that was Albert Einstein and the passage occurs in *Relativity: The General and Special Theory*, one of the seminal books in the history of physics. It could be objected that Einstein, in this instance is not writing "as a scientist" but that objection misses the point. Einstein is deliberately devising a style of writing whose purpose is to make a rather complex scientific idea available to a nonspecialist. He is primarily interested in his new theory, and hopes his readers will be too. What point would be served in writing as if he wasn't there? The question answers itself.

People who insist that the world consists of objective realities and (merely) subjective interpretations need to be reminded that such a neat division hasn't held for the best part of a hundred years. Our subjectivity is an inescapable part of being alive. Anyone who argues that we must take a god's eye view when we write on science—or anything else—is also arguing that he, or someone else, could be like a god. Even if we could rise to that giddy height what purpose would it serve? We are all flawed persons trying to make sense out of our world and communicating our discoveries and mistakes to human beings like ourselves. If we're to make any progress we need to learn a way communicating with each other using all our faculties, including our imperfections. No one among us, not even Einstein, will discover the "final truth" about anything.

"But writing isn't the same as speech," you might object. True. Writing is much more organized. Unlike most speech, it's a highly deliberated activity. But this is the real point: although your writing is different from your conversation it should still *sound* authentic. It should give the impression of a person expressing ideas in a clear and natural way. Whether you use the word "I" directly or convey your voice in an indirect way to your reader is a matter of context, not of correctness. The young author in the first pair of quotations about Mr. Pickwick uses both methods. To say that her second example, or the passage by Einstein's is not acceptable is to assert that a blind following of the rules is more important than common sense.

So far I've been conducting a polemic against the hourglass method and the problem of using the first person. That only takes us so far. What we need now is a positive strategy to guide us in all our written work. To arrive at that it's necessary to make a radical departure from the old model.

At this point I must add, very firmly, that I completely agree with all my colleagues who insist that a sound academic essay should have a coherent argument, it should use its sources responsibly, and it should honor the traditional norms of academic accountability. I'm not in any way championing a freeflowing impressionism or disjunctive reasoning (whatever that might mean). I'm encouraging clear responsible prose, which examines a topic in some depth, mounts a solid argument and is rounded off in a way that's logically entailed by its evidence.

*

This book is built around two central ideas. The first is this: *to write a worthwhile essay you have to be fully engaged.* That needs to be emphasized because so many essays seem to be written merely in order to "fulfill the requirement." The Hamlet essay is one example among countless thousands. That kind of writing never works. To write with conviction you have to plunge in, explore, take risks, make mistakes, be fully alert and stay involved. If you don't do that it will show immediately and you will hand in something that no one wants to read, including yourself.

The second central idea on which this book is based has much more subtle implications, though it can be stated simply: *an essay is a form of narration.* That might sound like a truism or an irrelevance. It's neither. On the contrary, it's germinal to our whole understanding of essay-writing. In order to reveal how, and why I want to introduce you to a new way of thinking which will profoundly alter the way you go about composing your essays.

FOUR:
What Lance Discovered

When Lance scrapped his opening paragraph and began his essay with something that came directly from his own experience, he did something quite significant. It deserves a close look.

Easily the most neglected quality in all writing is that, like a piece of music or a film, it can only happen in and through time. That might seem obvious, but the fact is that, for most people working on an essay in the hourglass form, the notion of time is almost irrelevant. That has serious consequences.

If language, whether spoken or written, is something which happens in and through time, it follows logically that the *order* in which we communicate our ideas is crucially important. You can see that quite easily if you reverse this sentence: *sentence this reverse you if easily quite that see can you.* You get nonsense because even a short sentence such as this contains quite a complex plot or story which doesn't reveal itself completely until the last word. The same thing applies to groups of sentences which form paragraphs, and paragraphs which form complete essays. They accumulate their total meaning only through time.

The original perpetrators of the hourglass model chose the name very deliberately. An hourglass, though it might be designed to *measure* time, is actually an object that exists in *space*. Even more to the point, it's reversible. What this all means when we sit down and try to use the hourglass model is that we force ourselves to think of ideas as parts of a static spatial diagram, not as a stream of evolving ideas.

Genuine writing lives in a subtle and invisible realm where thinking and listening are involved. That's why we recoil from a piece of writing that feels like an object or diagram. We seem to have a biological need: if a piece of writing is to hold our interest it must have a forward momentum. When that's broken we sense it as an almost physical blow. Lance stopped writing his first paragraph because his prose had become a stuck object. He found himself, once again, "writing by numbers."

Admittedly, those who wish to foist the hourglass model on young writers know that individual sentences in an essay must move through time. Yet, in their "rational diagramming" of the whole, they forget this fact and insist on a model which goes against the way human beings think, and the way our language actually works. That's why we are turned off by the Hamlet essay and its countless cousins. When we're forced to use such a model, as most of us have been, we have to fight against our own nature and the nature of language itself.

When Lance hit DELETE he knew he needed something very different from his usual practice. From the moment he found it, all the data he had so carefully gathered on his 4x6 cards began to form a pattern. He started to think of his essay as a *narration of ideas*. In other words, Lance discovered that special process which every writer has to rediscover, especially at those times your writing goes flat. You have to make your writing come alive and gather momentum.

Let's put it another way. Lance realized that in order to write naturally and fluently he had to begin thinking about words and sentences not as discrete units laid out in *space* but as part of a flow where ideas happen in *time*.

Everybody knows the drawing which shows a white wineglass centered on a black page. It takes a while to see that it is "really" two faces in profile. Learning a new way of looking at language and ideas is somewhat like that: we have to alter our angle of perception. It can be difficult, but the change is worth it. If you're willing to put up with a little discomfort, I can guarantee you it will make the whole enterprise of writing essays much more rewarding. Not only that: as you get used to it, as Lance did rather quickly, you will use your time more efficiently because, early on, you'll have a clear idea of where you're heading.

*

Let's go back to Lance and see what he wrote immediately after his new opening. You'll remember he began by recounting his experience of seeing a temple-garden as he wandered down a side-street in Kyoto. Then he suddenly thought of a passage in a book that he read the week before and jotted down on a notecard. That passage would provide a useful link. Here's how he continued:

> My curiosity was aroused by what I saw. Why such a dry, formal garden, and what was the relation between the garden and the monastery? Several weeks after my visit to Kyoto, I found an essay by J.P. Rawlingsby which began to give me an answer:
>
>> For the Japanese, the higher quality in landscape art is not a matter of "drama" and sudden dynamic modulations. Our Western tastes are not universal. We must remember that although we Occidentals might crave new aesthetic surprises to titillate our jaded senses, the wisdom of Japan proposes other values and priorities. There is a Zen saying: "Life tastes like water." For the Japanese sensibility, the moments of real perception are not magical or spectacular; they do not "blow the mind." They are experienced in a state of tranquility and meditation. The taste of water, they would say, if appreciated rightly, is very satisfying. It is a taste that is both mild and full.[1]

For most people old habits are stubborn, and Lance is no exception. As he writes this new first draft there's a tiny persistent voice in his head: *Your thesis should come about now.* Today he steadfastly ignores it because he wants to avoid what's happened in so many of his previous essays: early on they start to die. So he decides to go along with the natural run of his thought:

> What I want to examine in this essay are the implications of some of Rawlingsby's comparisons between Eastern and Western garden designs, and particularly what he means by "mild and full" in relation to temple-gardens. I also want to show that there is a very complex and somewhat paradoxical relationship between the growth of temple-gardens and the historical development of Zen Buddhism in Japan. I'll begin by giving a brief historical outline of how these things came together, particularly in the Kyoto region...

This little bridge-passage serves several purposes. It allows Lance to sketch out the broad concern of his essay. At the same time it provides him a way to escape the mind-numbing blow of a thesis statement. Third, it gives enough information to keep the reader both informed and curious. In other words, it allows Lance to continue developing his ideas in time. It's very important to note that he does have a thesis and he could write it down, at least in rough form. For the moment, though, he wants it to hover over his essay, a little unformed, coloring everything he has to say but not making itself overt. While he holds it there in suspension it has great power, which he will later express at the appropriate place.

What Lance did in his new opening freed his imagination. He discovered that writing an essay is somewhat like constructing a short story. Whereas a short story has a **plot** which is set in motion by its **characters**, an essay consists of an overall **argument** which is articulated through its **ideas.** This was another important discovery because it helped him arrange his ideas in a process that keeps developing, as in the plot of a short story, until the very last word.

After his last bridge passage Lance had numerous choices. He wanted to show what he'd promised, namely, "the complex and somewhat paradoxical relationship between temple-gardens and the historical development of Zen." He saw that in this essay the simplest strategy would be to arrange all the relevant material in a sequence which goes from less important to more important. His material will include:

—A brief description of the earliest temple-gardens in the region;

—An account of the growth of temple-gardens at several crucial points in Japanese history;

—A study of the different changes in Buddhist beliefs and practices over the period that provide us with evidence of the nature and purpose of temple-gardens;

—An account of the peculiar tension between the common Buddhist notion of the desirability of emptiness as a spiritual condition, and of aesthetic beauty, as expressed in outward forms such as rocks, plants, gravel and buildings, and so on;

—A brief discussion of recent architectural trends in Japan as they affect the design of new and refurbished temples and their gardens.

After that, when he's given all he needs in order to show the "complex relationship" he spoke of earlier, he can end by unleashing the full power of his thesis statement, which brings his essay to a proper conclusion. This is how he ends his first draft:

> Unlike formal gardens in the West, temple-gardens in Japan, as I have tried to show in this paper, have both an obvious and a hidden function. Well before the coming of Zen to Japan the Japanese were consummate gardeners. What Zen brought to the Japanese garden was a sense of austerity and bareness. These gardens are a space where one can "empty one's mind," which in Zen (but perhaps not in the West) is a desirable thing. At the same time the bareness of the temple garden promotes a kind of dialogue with the more colorful and decorative gardens one finds elsewhere in Japan, sometimes in great abundance. The two different types of gardens define and complement each other. They can even be said to depend on each other for their meaning. Lovers may consort in public-gardens, but they do not usually do so in temple-gardens. Temple-gardens are spaces for meditation where one should stand alone. So a lover or spouse might go to a temple-garden in private and, in doing so, bring back from the "empty place" a small breath of Zen wisdom to the social world where most of us spend most of our time.

Now that the broad lines and many of the significant details of his essay have been captured in this first draft, Lance will spend the next few days fine-tuning it, reassured by the knowledge that the essay is almost there. He won't have to struggle with its basic form, only with the details.

With this approach Lance is able to set down an authentic expression of his own thought, and it has a voice—his voice. He would be quite comfortable reading it before a live audience because he knows it "works."

At this point in Lance's career the sacred cows have vanished.

*

The model of writing I will examine in the chapter that follows the *First Interlude* gives a more specific annotated example of the new approach that Lance has twigged intuitively. Following that are five more alternative models which you may find useful in your written work in college and beyond. However, they're all based on the assumption that you have a good grasp of the foundational new model I've called ILIAD, for reasons which I hope will become obvious.

First Interlude

The Hidden Power of Free-Writing

Usually, "free-writing" refers to the kind of warm-up exercise in which you fasten on something vivid in your mind. The aim is to write fast, without worrying about being "correct." Such exercises are often prompted by a trigger such as: *When I dove in…* or, *the thing I like most about…* What matters most is that you keep writing. If you dislike the exercise you can write about that, and give the reasons why, but in any case it's most important keep your head down and let go.

Sometimes what you uncover in such exercises is very revealing. It can be particularly valuable for people who dislike writing because they discover that they *can* say something important and may find that writing is much more interesting than they'd imagined. The chief aim of free-writing is to get used to the physical act of writing as a natural activity, so if you can make that breakthrough a good deal of your apprehension and resistance will begin to fall away.

Although free-writing is useful as an exercise for all writers, when we consider its place in academic writing a slight shift of gears is called for. Lance's experience illustrates that. Lance had done a good deal of free-writing in a short story class, but it never occurred to him that it could have any place in his academic work. That morning he discovered it could. Without thinking about it consciously, this is what he did: *he found a way of connecting his personal experience with the topic he'd chosen to write about.* He'd seen a good number of temple-gardens on his trips to Japan and he decided to use that experience *directly* in order to get started. That was his "trigger" and it allowed him to move from personal observation to matters which are "out there." In other words, although his topic sprang from, and was brought to life by personal experience, it went well beyond it.

Please note that if you adopt the kind of approach Lance used to get yourself started you don't have to stick literally to your opening in your later drafts. As your essay develops you may find something much more suitable as an introduction. Your "free-writing" is a stratagem to get yourself beyond being stuck. Here's another example from the preliminary draft of an essay on the Philosophy of Law:

> "Well, he only done what he had to do—and that's right—in't it?" I heard this come out the mouth of an old lady on a London tube-train on my first day in that city and I never thought it might point to something very interesting about the way we judge and sentence people. Whether she was aware of it or not, the speaker was pointing to one of the central legal puzzles of our time. It's so far-reaching that to approach it properly would mean looking at the findings of experts in many fields. Obviously, even if I had the ability, that would take years, so in order to begin I will have to restrict my study to the more narrow framework of present law.
>
> The question behind what the old lady said can be stated like this: to what degree is our behavior in any given situation determined by things outside our control? That question slides over into another one, which is very important in many criminal proceedings: how far should we be held responsible for our actions when we commit a serious crime? To give to that question clear focus I'll deal with a recent case of arson, (Tolland *v.* the State of Kentucky, March–April, 2006) to see how the question played out in the trial.

The words of the old lady on the tube-train had preoccupied the author for a long time for reasons he didn't quite understand. It was only when he began to think about what she said in relation to his chosen topic that the reason he recalled the incident vividly became clear. *But he had to write about it before its full implication emerged.* Once he got going, the link became firmer and he was able to proceed in a way that seemed natural and liberating.

To many the above example may seem an entirely unsuitable opening for an academic essay. It is nonetheless the way most writers start out. *They write to discover.* The poet, W. H. Auden once put this very succinctly: *How can I know what I think before I see what I say?* If you go about your essays in this spirit your writing becomes an exploration, not simply a "rational" compiling of data. The distinction between "academic" and what is normally called "creative writing" falls away and you will begin to experience your essay as something new, something that can bring you and your readers pleasure, as well as information. When you abandon the old idea that your writing has to be "special" and "formal" and, instead, begin with your own perceptions and experiences, your words will catch fire.

PART II

ILIAD
or
A Model for All Seasons

FIVE:
The Structure of ILIAD

The ILIAD model for essays is not a fixed form. It's far more useful to think of it as a *strategy*. Though you can regard it as a five-stage process, it bears only a superficial resemblance to the models you've probably been using. Nonetheless it's useful to set down the five stages in a schematic way before we see how they function as a whole:

INTRODUCTION
LINK
INDICATING THE THESES, STATING YOUR INTENTION
ADVANCING THE ARGUMENT
DEDUCTION / CONCLUSION

Here's a brief description of each stage:

INTRODUCTION

The primary purpose of the Introduction, especially in the first draft, is to get *you* going. What's the first thing that comes to mind when you muse deeply on your topic? It could be something that comes directly from your own experience, as it was for Lance. Whatever it is, don't question it, get it down. Its purpose in your overall design will reveal itself very soon. Remember at this stage it's not something cast in stone. You may want to scrap it later but, for now, run with it.

Link

This is the bridge that allows you to move beyond the specific thing you wrote about in your Introduction and show how it bears on your topic as a whole.

Indicating the Thesis, Stating the Intention

At this point your reader will want to know two things: *what* is your essay trying to show and *how* will you proceed? In the old method this the place where you usually set down your thesis. As I have shown, and as we all know, when you do that immediately you will have to fight hard not to turn the rest of your paper into an anticlimax. You will have given your conclusion away. "But my reader will want to know something very clear about what I'm doing." These apparently contradictory ideas are both true and they can be reconciled. In this new way of structuring, this is the point where, without impeding the forward flow of your narrative, you give a strong *indication* of your thesis, without stating it in full. This might seem very difficult at first because you are not used to it, but the illustration in the sample essay below will show you one way of getting round the difficulty of the old thesis habit.

Advancing the Argument

There are many ways of doing this. The sample essay shows one way. There are five more examples in the later section on Alternative Forms. The chief thing to remember is that all good essays are consequential and they hold the reader's attention until the very last word. If you keep that in mind your essay will stay alive.

Deduction/ Conclusion

Having fulfilled implicitly, in the body of your essay, the purpose you indicated at the outset, you will want to round off your argument by making your conclusion more explicit by drawing all your main ideas together and stating your *full thesis* (or tentative thesis, or summarizing question.) This is what we, your readers, have been waiting for.

Sample Essay: The Model In Action

Jan Smeaton, a sophomore in Modern American History 209: The Politics of the Cold War, in consultation with her teacher, has chosen to write an essay (2,500–3,000 words) on the topic of "Robert Oppenheimer as an American Prometheus."

The emphasis in this course is a study of the main events and figures in American History in the period of the Cold War. Students were asked to choose early in the term an important American figure through whom some of the political tensions of that period can be understood.

Here, with explanatory sidenotes, is the somewhat abbreviated text of Jan's second draft.

Jan's text (as yet untitled)

In early June 1949 Robert Oppenheimer was required to testify before the Joint Commission on Atomic Energy. One person on the committee of enquiry, Lewis Strauss, had immense power behind the scenes. Oppenheimer thought that, scientifically, Strauss was ill informed and his fear that isotopes could be used by foreign powers to generate atomic energy was without foundation. Strauss, on his part, had had serious reservations about Oppenheimer for more than a year, and he was convinced that isotopes presented a threat to national security. When his time came to testify on this matter this is what Oppenheimer said:

> No one can force me to say that you cannot use these isotopes for atomic energy; in fact, you do. You can use a bottle of beer for atomic energy. In fact, you do. (1)

Shortly after he added this:

> My own rating of isotopes in this broad sense is that they are far less important than electronic devices. But far more important than, let us say, vitamins, somewhere in between. (2)

Several of Oppenheimer's friends and colleagues in the Hearing Room realized that this was a significant moment even though Oppenheimer himself made light of it. Years later, David Lilenthal recalling Strauss' reaction, said: "There was a look of hatred there that you don't see very often on a man's face." Later events proved that Strauss never forgot the incident, nor did he ever forgive Oppenheimer for this public act of humiliation.

A number of things can be noted even from a small incident such as this.

INTRODUCTION

In her reading, Jan was very struck by one person who had an extreme dislike of Oppenheimer and, recalling a rather dramatic moment in an important hearing, and without concerning herself for the moment about its broader implications, she sets it down. She's relying on a firm instinct that it will provide a useful springboard for her essay.

LINK

Jan now thinks hard about how this incident might lead into her essay as a whole, and pretty quickly she comes up with something that can be stated quite simply. Note that Jan is continuing to think of the forward-

(Jan makes her link by giving a detailed analysis of Oppenheimer's faults and virtues as a scientist and as a leader of the Manhattan Project, pointing out that, in particular, that he was a great friend and party-giver but also, at times arrogant and dismissive, especially with strangers. She intimates that the faults in his very complex personality almost certainly had a great deal to do with his final downfall. She then continues, with this):

moving aspects of her essay. For example, the opening words of her first sentence in this link, and the word *this* maintains the narrative flow in her writing.

My purpose in this paper is to study some of the central characteristics of Oppenheimer as a scientist and intellectual leader who was politically involved in some of the most troubling questions of his time.

Oppenheimer has often been referred to as an "American Prometheus." In fact, that ascription is the subtitle of the book by Kai Bird and Martin J. Sherwin, from which I've drawn of good deal of my information in this paper. In at least two ways that characterization is very apt. First, Oppenheimer has attained a legendary position in our history. He was a figure who like Prometheus, can justifiably be called "larger than life." His achievements are monumental and are deservedly looked on with awe. Second, he certainly brought mankind a "gift of fire" in his case in an almost unimaginably destructive form. So, as with his Greek counterpart, the word "gift," has to be taken with a certain irony. Yet in spite of the similarities between these two "heroic figures" what I want to show in this essay is that, in Oppenheimer's case we have to ask the question "Does the title quite fit?"

INDICATING THE THESIS

Jan has, to this point, not set down her thesis. So right now she has a problem to solve, the one which I alluded to earlier. She wants to give her reader a clear sense of the essential *substance* of her essay and at the same time keep her essay open as an unfolding intellectual narrative. Note, again, that she is keeping the *full* statement of her thesis until she has assembled her major points. This is her ace in the hole.

How to stop your papers from killing you (and me)

I want to address that question by looking at four things: Oppenheimer's work as a physicist and as a leader on the Los Alamos Project; his somewhat baffling and enduring association with the Communist Party; his long quarrel with, and ultimate betrayal by Edward Teller; and, last, his conflict with Lewis Strauss.

INTENTION

It's doubtful whether the Los Alamos project could even have gotten launched, let alone been brought to its terrifying, and successful conclusion, without Oppenheimer. Not only was he one of the most able physicists of his generation, he was a very able manager of even the most trivial details of the Los Alamos community. This included his handling of General Groves, who was appointed to manage the whole enterprise. Groves, who could be difficult to deal with, had enormous respect for Oppenheimer who gained his confidence at their first meeting. In that he never wavered. (4)

First major point: Oppenheimer as a scientist and leader.

(see Bird, corroborate with McMillan, get pages)

This points up a very important distinction concerning our two "heroes." Prometheus, for all we know, was a lone figure. He had no advisors, and no one to be responsible for but himself. Oppenheimer, though he stood out at Los Alamos in many ways, was very much a member of a brilliant team. He would have been incapable of solving some of the chief problems of harnessing fissionable material for detonation were it not for his fellow-physicists. Yet he was able to keep peace even with some of the more fractious members of his circle, and particularly with Edward Teller, by a combination of charm and tolerance which is well beyond the capacity of most leaders. It was this double gift that provided the essential ingredients for the success of the whole wartime experiment. (5) *(Bird and MacMillan, cite pages)*

For this reason Oppenheimer's long association with the Communist Party is particularly puzzling. Russia and Communism were both very troubling for the United States Government and for the populace as whole. One of the driving forces behind the whole push to "get the bomb" was not only to beat Germany but, particularly, the U.S.S.R who, by all current accounts, was also very advanced in its work on fission. Many people considered Russia, who was an "ally," to be as dangerous as Germany in this respect.

Second major point: Oppenheimer's association with the Communist Party

Oppenheimer was never a full member of the C.P. nor was ever officially indicted for being a communist. At the same time, there was no doubt that he was sympathetic toward some of the central ideas of Communism and he did make financial contributions to the Party. Yet, for years he was able to hold himself aloof from criticism. It was as if his almost legendary status protected him from the persecution suffered by his brother and other communist sympathizers with whom he was intimately involved. (6) *(Explanatory footnote needed)*. A curious puzzle concerning his motives remains. Oppenheimer, at any time, could have allayed any official doubts about his "communist past" by simply making a public renunciation. He knew what the Government and the country as a whole thought about it. Yet for some reason he chose to ignore all that. Maybe he considered his political beliefs his own business, maybe he was naïve about its implications, or maybe—as with his insulting of Strauss at the hearing on isotopes—in certain matters he simply didn't mind if he offended people. He never tried to disguise or to apologize for his communist sympathies. In fact he rarely spoke or wrote about them, so perhaps his true motives will never be known.

If the Los Alamos story and the search by Oppenheimer and his team for the ultimate weapon to end the war was a drama with Oppenheimer as the chief protagonist, the chief villain was Edward Teller. Oppenheimer battled with him continuously over one major question, about which they were both equally stubborn. Teller saw himself as only peripherally involved with the uranium and the plutonium bombs, but he never wavered in his ambition to build the so-called H (or Hydrogen) Bomb. Teller knew that such a bomb could wipe out millions. Oppenheimer for two reasons resisted him at every turn: in his judgment the pursuit of such a bomb deflected from his mandate to produce a weapon that would end the war. More important, though, were Oppenheimer's moral objections to such a bomb. For him the uranium and, later, the plutonium bomb were almost unthinkable "gifts" to mankind. By a factor of thousands, the H-bomb far exceeded what was needed and the very idea of such a weapon was, for him, totally unconscionable.

Jan's third and fourth major points, the conflict with Edward Teller and the role of Lewis Strauss in the revoking of his security clearance, and his final downfall, are the heart of her essay and I have at this point transcribed her draft in full.

Some notion of his attitude can be gauged from his reaction after the first test explosion in the desert. Quoting the *Bhagavad Gita* he was reputed to have said: "Now I am become Death, destroyer of worlds." (8) *(Explanatory footnote)*

In any case, for these two reasons Oppenheimer kept Teller at bay, but Teller used every opportunity to curry favor with the President and others in power in order promote his aim. When it came to the climax in the hearings over the question of whether Oppenheimer was to keep his security clearance this conflict was crucial. Perhaps even more than the assiduous backroom work of Strauss, Teller's testimony was the deciding factor in his fate.

Strauss' part in the "play" was, nonetheless, sinister and decisive. Strauss never approved of Oppenheimer, so, unlike Teller, who was a fellow-scientist, his role was somewhat different. His vendetta was personal, though being a clever bureaucrat, he rationalized that in seeking the demise of Oppenheimer he was hopefully fulfilling the wish of the President and protecting National Security. Be that as it may, Strauss' influence in the "trial" that finally brought Oppenheimer down was all-pervasive and very tellingly orchestrated. As it's quite complicated I will summarize the major points.

From the outset of the trial Strauss saw to it that the legal structures brought to bear against Oppenheimer were so loaded that the outcome was almost preordained. He virtually chose Oppenheimer's lawyer, designed the format of the trial, and chose a prosecuting lawyer who was equally zealous to destroy Oppenheimer once and for all. Finally, having spent years promoting his own ambition in this respect, Strauss cleverly denied Oppenheimer the chance to defend himself or explain his motives.

As the trial moved toward its climax, various associates of Oppenheimer were brought in to testify on his behalf. Many of them spoke well of him but, in this context, their testimony was shunted aside. However, when it came to Edward Teller the whole scene changed.

In aggressive cross-examination on April 28th, 1954 *(check date)*, Roger Robb, the appointed prosecutor, put Teller in the chair and asked him: "Is it your intention in anything that you are about to testify to, to suggest that Dr. Oppenheimer is disloyal to the United States?"

Teller's immediate reply was, "I think it would be presumptuous and wrong on my part if I would in any way analyze his motives. But I have always assumed, and now assume, that he is loyal to the United States. I believe this, and I shall believe it until I see very conclusive proof to the opposite."

Robb pressed Teller further: "Now, a question which is a corollary of that. Do you or do you not believe that Dr. Oppenheimer is a security risk?" This was Teller's opportunity, at last, to have his say, and he grasped it:

"In a great number of cases I have seen Dr. Oppenheimer act—I understood that Dr. Oppenheimer acted in a way which was exceedingly difficult for me to understand. I thoroughly disagreed with him in numerous issues, and his actions, frankly, appeared to me confused and complicated. To this extent, I feel that I would like to see the vital interests of this country in hands which I understand better and could therefore trust more."

Chairman Gray then cross-questioned Teller on this issue, who continued: "If it is a question of wisdom and judgment, as demonstrated by his action since 1945, then I would say one would be wiser not to grant clearance."

Teller then tried to soften this blow: "I must say that I am myself a little bit confused on this issue, particularly as it refers to a person of Oppenheimer's prestige and influence. May I limit myself to these comments?" (9)

The damage was done. Teller's testimony was a deathblow: Oppenheimer had been hanged by one of his fellow-scientists. A few months later Oppenheimer security clearance was rescinded just one day before it was due to expire.

(In her thesis statement, in which she has to come to a conclusion about whether Oppenheimer was an "American Prometheus," Jan has to give a complex answer because the question is a difficult one. What follows is a somewhat abbreviated version of her final paragraphs.)

Much more can be said about Oppenheimer's very complex career and personality. As I said at the outset, like Prometheus, he was a figure who could

DEDUCTION AND FULL STATEMENT OF THESIS

be justly described as "larger than life." He was a focus for some of the most troubling scientific and political questions of his time. His discoveries and what they brought to the world still trouble us. However I believe that the title "An American Prometheus," by which he is often known, needs a closer look. Prometheus stole fire from the gods, was bound to a stake for his crime, and later released by Herakles. His motives were somewhat obscure. Oppenheimer did not steal anything; he had to fulfill a scientific duty and he was never released from his bondage. Quite the opposite; he died a dishonored man. From the beginnings of the Los Alamos Project his abilities as a scientist and his loyalty to his country in a time of acute danger came together and forced him into a position which, in major ways, ran against his conscience.

Yet, his duty was, from the start, very clear: he had to find a decisive weapon of immense destructiveness or, as he believed, see his country destroyed by one. It was a choice that terrified him, and he couldn't escape it. That brings me to this conclusion: Although he resembled Prometheus in a number of ways his ultimate fate was more like that of a classical Greek tragic hero. That parallel, however, requires some important qualifications. It's useful here to turn to Aristotle's definition of tragedy:

> Tragedy, then, is an imitation of an action that is serious, complete, and of a certain magnitude; in language embellished with each kind of artistic ornament, the several kinds being found in the separate parts of the play; in the form of action, not of narrative; with incidents arousing pity

Having fulfilled her stated intention to look at the four main points she mentioned Jan is now ready to draw her study of Oppenheimer to its conclusion.

and fear wherewith to accomplish its catharsis of such emotions.... *(my underlining)* (10)

Considered in this light, the "tragedy" of J. Robert Oppenheimer makes an interesting contrast with those of the heroes of Greek tragedy. His story—which was not an "imitation" but a sequence of real historical events—was clearly "of a certain magnitude" and it certainly arouses "pity" and "fear." But it does not, I would argue, achieve "catharsis" in the audience. Oppenheimer's "audience" is us and we know the "play" is still going on right now.

There are other differences. The Greek heroes could not escape their "fate" because it was predestined by the gods. Oppenheimer's fate occurred in a world of technology and scientists and politicians and war; it was conditioned by the dynamic historical forces that gathered and tightened around him. They were the modern composite "god" and they were—along with the very powerful figures of Edward Teller and Strauss—what finally brought him down. What makes Oppenheimer stand out was that, like the Greek heroes, he was acutely aware of his total situation. He knew, all along what he had to fight, and he knew fairly early on that he would probably fall. But what brought him down was not "fate" or an obscure edict of "the gods." He was caught in a web woven by an ambitious fellow-scientist and a ruthless politician, by himself, and by the perilous historical circumstances in which they all lived.

In the final count, then, though he had something in common with the heroes of Greek tragedy and with Prometheus, those comparisons, as I have tried to show, are in important ways somewhat misleading.

A Note on Jan's Footnotes: Jan will have to acknowledge her chief sources in her bibliography and, in some cases, add explanatory notes. For example, Oppenheimer apparently did not quote the *Bhagavad Gita* out loud at the first test in the desert, although he claims he "thought" it at that time; he first uttered those words in a much later interview. That, and several more points will need to be included, as well the bibliographical details for all her footnotes. These things are absolutely essential. In this second draft, to make my main concerns clearer, I wanted to emphasize Jan's overall structuring of her paper.

A Last Word on ILIAD

Jan found her early drafts relatively easy to write not only because she was familiar with her topic and very interested in Oppenheimer's fate. She also employed a design that allowed a natural development of her material. She still has some work to do, but it's essentially the kind of cleaning up and fine-tuning that any worthwhile piece of writing requires. At no point has the essay been, in its design, a deep puzzle for her, because, like Lance, she started with something very alive in her imagination and found a way of helping it unfold.

ILIAD, seen as an overall strategy, rather than as a fixed framework, can be used in a wide variety of circumstances. You might see this approach merely as a preliminary stage in your growth as a writer and be looking for something more advanced. If that's the case, the approaches in the later section on Alternative Forms should provide you with some challenging possibilities.

SIX:
A Note on Writing in the Sciences

Roughly speaking, there are two kinds of scientific writing. The first covers the kind of specialized exposition we find in lab reports, experimental findings, and research papers. All of these have strict conventions which have been made clear by your teachers in science classes. For that reason I won't deal with them here. The method of writing essays I've been advocating so far will be of minimal use in these specialist areas. There is, however, another kind of scientific writing which could be called "writing *about* science." Much of it takes the form of an examination not so much of the technical findings of a scientific discovery or experiment but of their implications. Many first-rate scientists, such as Albert Einstein, with the aim of making their highly specialized work more available to lay readers, have written quite voluminously in this field. In fact, for people who are not familiar with the professional languages and procedures of science, such writing is the only way we learn what scientists do.

This second kind of writing often contains a good deal of highly technical information. The challenge for the writer is how to make that information informative *and* readable, and all I've been saying so far in this book is highly relevant. Poor writers in scientific fields often work on the assumption that if they just present "the facts" they will have fulfilled the essential requirements. Skilled writers work very differently; they realize that facts don't really come alive until they are brought together in a comprehensible pattern. The way that facts are presented is therefore every bit as important as their accuracy. Such writers—whether or not they are consciously aware of it—are concerned, like those in the humanities, to make their work what I have called "a form of engaged narration."

Here are some examples by scientists of this second kind of science writing. As you read them you will notice that they have something in common:

> To hold its own in the struggle for existence, every species of animal must have a regular source of food, and if it happens to live on other animals its survival may be very delicately balanced. The hunter cannot exist without the hunted; if the latter should perish from the earth, the former would, too. When the hunted also prey on some of the hunters, the matter may become complicated.
>
> This is nowhere better illustrated than in the insect world. Think of the complexity of a situation such as the following. There is a certain wasp, *Pimpla inquisitor*, whose larvae feed on the larvae of the tussock moth. *Pimpla inquisitor* larvae in turn serve as food for the larvae of a second wasp, and the latter in their turn nourish still a third wasp. What subtle balance between fertility and mortality in the case of each of these four species to prevent the extinction of all of them! An excess of mortality over fertility in a single member of the group would ultimately wipe out all four.
>
> This is not a unique case. The two great orders of insects, Hymenoptera and Diptera, are full of such examples of interrelationship. And the spiders (which are not insects but a member of a separate order of arthropods) are also victims and killers of insects.
>
> —Alexander Petrunkevitch, *The Spider and the Wasp*, p. 1

> At any rate, to continue with this "history," Paul Dirac, using the theory of relativity, made a relativistic theory of the electron that did not take completely into account all the effects of the electron's interaction with light. Dirac's theory said that an electron had a magnetic moment—something like the force of a little magnet that had a strength of exactly 1 in certain units. Then in about 1948 it was discovered in experiments that the actual number was closer to 1.00118 (with an uncertainty of about 3 on the last digit). It was known, of course, that electrons in-

teract with light, so some small correction was expected. It was also expected that this correction would be understandable from the new theory of quantum electrodynamics. But when it was calculated, instead of 1.00118 the result was infinity— which is wrong, experimentally!
—Richard P. Feynman, *QED, The Strange Theory of Light and Matter*, p. 6

The Antarctic pink and Antarctic bundle grass are the only two flowering plants in the Antarctic. By contrast, there are over a hundred species of flowering plants in the comparable north polar latitudes and, in life's greatest eloquence of diversity, the Amazon Basin, there are fifty thousand species. The patch I am examining is as complex as Antarctic terrestrial ecosystems get. Consider this: one leaf of an Amazonian palm—one leaf out of trillions in that 3,000-kilometer-wide swatch of tropical forest—may have living on top of it more species of mosses, fungi, lichens, protozoans, mites, and insects than are found in the whole continent of Antarctica.
—David G. Campbell, *The Crystal Desert*, p. 57

I said earlier that these examples have one thing in common. Actually, they have two. In every case you can feel the presence of an individual person, a style—what has sometimes been called a "voice." Their writers have not tried to conceal their identities, nor have they flaunted them. They all write in a way which, for them, feels natural. Feynman, who was a very colorful person and lecturer with his "At any rate..." opening, is somewhat more breezy than most writers in science. Campbell, by using the first person, places himself and us in the situation he is describing, and Petrunkevitch, who is clearly fascinated by the processes he is describing, keeps himself out of his prose and lets the story speak for itself. In all three cases the writing is *personal* in the special sense I have been using that word. The author is "there," thoroughly involved and engaged.

What follows from that involvement is that their writing is *readable*. That adjective needs to be unpacked. Put it this way: when our writing contains technical details we must pace them so that our audience *can un-*

derstand them as they read. Our readers should not have to make frequent pauses. You attain the skill of pacing through trial-and-error, by testing your writing voice on different audiences, some who read it silently, and some who hear you read it aloud, preferably without a text. Ask them for their reactions. Did they fully understand what you're saying? If not, you'll have to make the appropriate adjustments in *pace* and *density*.

The question of voice in your own writing is not as simple as it sounds because it's not really your voice that's transcribed on the page. You can prove this very easily by making a recording when you're speaking as coherently as you can. It will have a *relation* to your best writing but it will not be identical with it. What you are really looking for when writing about science, or anything else, is a *writing style* which sounds as if you were speaking. A useful stratagem is to imagine you are writing for your peers, who are interested in what you are doing but not well-versed in the technicalities. Your aim is to make the individual items and the overall pattern come alive. You have to put yourself in your audience's shoes. The three writers above have shared facts which I, for one, didn't know before, and they've done that in a pleasing way. They make it all sound straightforward and spontaneous. It isn't. They had to learn how to do that and, like playing a piano or guitar naturally, it takes practice.

One way of learning to write well about scientific matters, or anything else, is to take a writer whose work you admire. If you slow down and study one of your favorite passages you'll lean a great deal. How is an important idea introduced? How are the chief emphases made? What special skills keep the facts alive? If you can isolate the way your authors deploy these skills you can use them in your own work, modifying them as you need. This will make you a more conscious editor of your own work. All artists have done that, from the time of the cave-painters to Jackson Pollock, from Homer to Dickens to Stephen King. *So that's how you do it*, the apprentice artist says, *I think I'll try that*. There's nothing shameful about learning skills from others. In fact, we don't really have any choice. Think about how you learned to walk, and to speak. You had some skilled models. Though I'm arguing throughout this book that writing should be a pleasurable exploration it is, at the same time, a demanding challenge. We need all the help we can get.

PART III
FIVE ALTERNATIVE FORMS

The False Thesis
Dialectics and Dialogues
Approaching Sideways
Prismatic Composition
Mixed Forms

A PRELIMINARY NOTE

All good essays—academic or otherwise—are creatures after their own kind and it's therefore impossible to provide a full account of their structures. What I've done here is to isolate a number of strategies that successful essay writers have adopted and which may give you some ideas for your next paper.

SEVEN:
The False Thesis

I claimed earlier that it's almost impossible to write an interesting essay using the usual model. There is, however at least one exception: you use that model, but for a very different purpose. When you write an hourglass essay you are, usually, a passive servant of someone else's form. In this next example, Rick Valento, a senior English major, wanting to try something different for his final essay in Modern American Poetry, chooses to play with the old form in a way that suits his purposes for this occasion. His paper is tentatively called *That Other Road: Study of a Poem by Robert Frost*. Here's a shortened version of what he hopes will be his final draft:

> Most people know this poem but because I need to concentrate closely on a few details, I'll give the text in full:
>
> **The Road Not Taken**
> Two roads diverged in a yellow wood,
> And sorry I could not travel both
> And be one traveler, long I stood
> And looked down one as far as I could
> To where it bent in the undergrowth;
>
> Then took the other, as just as fair
> And having perhaps the better claim,
> Because it was grassy and wanted wear;

> Though, as for that, the passing there
> Had worn them really about the same
>
> And both that morning equally lay
> In leaves no step had trodden black.
> Oh, I kept the first for another day!
> Yet knowing how way leads on to way,
> I doubted if I should ever come back.
>
> I shall be telling this with a sigh
> Somewhere ages and ages hence:
> Two roads diverged in a wood, and I—
> I chose the one less traveled by,
> And that has made all the difference.[4]

The speaker in the poem is an older, maybe middle-aged man, looking back on a choice he made some time ago (the poem doesn't specify exactly how long ago) and describing the nature of that choice. The metaphor of the divided road is an obvious one. In fact it's a cliché. What matters is what Frost does with it. To put it very briefly, the speaker is recounting how he stood at a fork of the road and, after considering both possibilities, decides on the second or "other" road, giving as his reason that it was "grassy and wanted wear" and, in the last stanza, claiming that it was that choice "that has made all the difference."

Rick continues by giving an account of the accepted reading of the poem in which Frost is a rugged individual who makes a choice between two very different roads and decides on the one which is "less traveled by." Then he makes a surprising move which he'd been planning all along:

> In spite of its almost universal acceptance there's a huge problem in this reading of the poem: when we look closely at the words in the text this interpretation will not work because it is contradicted by what the words of the poem actually say. The paraphrase of the poem I gave earlier is not only misleading, it's a flagrant misreading of the words on

the page. Admittedly, the first few lines of the second stanza seem to support the usual interpretation:

> ...Then took the other as just as fair
> Because it was grassy and wanted wear

So far so good, but the lines that immediately follow, though quietly stated, say something very different:

> Though, as for that, *the passing there*
> *Had worn them really about the same*
> *And both that morning equally lay*
> *In leaves no step had trodden black.* (my italics)

In a careful examination Rick shows why the accepted interpretation is flawed, and supports his contention by giving other examples that reveal that, in spite of his apparent simplicity, Frost is often a trickier poet than he seems. Then he points to a tiny detail in the last stanza:

> I shall be telling this with a sigh
> Somewhere ages and ages hence:
> *Two roads diverged in a wood, and I—*
> *I chose the one less traveled by,*
> *And that has made all the difference.* (my italics and emphases)

The placement of the colon after "hence" is crucial. What follows it immediately is a quotation, not from the speaker of the poem in the present, but from what he predicts *he will be saying* somewhere "ages and ages hence," perhaps to a grandchild. In other words, what is being said in these lines is not continuous with the voice in the rest of the poem. The colon reveals that there are not two, but three time-frames in the poem: the present, from where the poem as a whole is being told, the past where the speaker made his choice between the roads, and the future from where he will tell about the choice he made a very long time ago. Put another way, the words that follow the colon are the substance of what he will say when he's reminiscing in some unspecified future time. And Frost is implying that, when he later explains the choice of road he made that day, he will be telling a fib.

Having developed an argument which goes counter to the widely-accepted reading of the poem, Rick now moves naturally to his conclusion:

> This reading of the poem yields a very different meaning from the one we have been used to. If my interpretation is sound, Frost is not only poking fun at the speaker's need to make up a story about his past, he's also possibly having an affectionate dig at this common human habit. We make our choices blind, between alternatives which are "really about the same," but because this doesn't make an interesting story we dress the differences up to show how luck, taste, temperament, artistic calling, or whatever, make our choices into something much more special than they really are. Such a reading also makes the last line of the poem one of the most complex in Frost's work and perhaps in the whole of modern poetry. Read one way, it's a kind of tautological nonsense because, as we know, any choice makes "all the difference." Yet we can't even be certain of that because we can only make one choice at a time. The experiment of life, with its many choices, has no "control." Read in this way, the line dissolves into itself and is outrageously funny because there was no deep significance in the speaker's choice in the woods *except the one he will invent when he tells about it later*. The choice will gather significance because, and only because, in hindsight, it will allow him, to use his own words, to "strike a line of purpose" across his experience. But that "purpose" is something he will *invent* many years later. The writer of the poem, and this is definitely Robert Frost, is perhaps pointing to the fact that all of us, in telling about our past, will very likely give an account which is on occasion proud, firm, entirely human, and deluded.

It will be obvious now why I've called this alternative the "false thesis." Rick does give a thesis near the beginning. Then, by a very swift reversal, he undermines it and uses it as a whetstone on which to hone a totally different reading of the poem. This strategy upsets our formal expectations of correct behavior in an essay. Done skillfully, it can make for a very readable essay because, as in a good story, it catches us off guard.

The false thesis has many variants. For example, you may wish not to overturn completely the thesis you've stated in your opening, but to modify it in some significant way. Or you might overturn it completely, then grant that you've been too severe and show there's more in the original thesis than you at first acknowledged.

Needless to say, the "false thesis"—whichever variant you use—is not an alternative you should employ regularly. In fact, it's not a sound idea to use any of these alternative models as a staple because that will only take you back into the prison from which you've been trying to escape. Each essay we write should be shaped to fit the nature of its topic and the way we want to approach it. Rick has found a suitable way of making his major point *on this particular occasion*. In his next paper, he may want to try something quite different.

EIGHT:
Dialogues and Dialectics

Some writers prefer to shine a steady light on their topic. Some prefer to set things up dramatically by playing two opposing ideas or interpretations against each other. You have to follow the impulses of your own temperament. If you're drawn to a more dramatic type of presentation the following will give you something to consider.

Vinnie is a senior pursuing a double major in History and English. For her final essay, she is required to write a paper on a topic that bridges both her major fields. She's been wrestling all year with a challenging puzzle and wants to have crack at it. Well into writing her first draft, she came across two quotations by two different authorities on her topic which spoke precisely to her own dilemma. She decides to use these sharply contrasting quotations as an immediate way into her essay. This is a somewhat abbreviated version of her working draft:

Mr. Pickwick and President Reagan:
Notes on a Real or Fictional Problem

It will be useful to begin with two very different notions of what historians do:

> 1. The historian's prime responsibility is to his facts. Admittedly, facts can come from a great variety of sources—official documents, letters, eyewitness accounts, headstones, county records, broadcasts, television and film-footage—and much more, but, whatever his sources might be, they are all the historian can work with...

The author, E.L. Malmsby in his book (*The Disciplines of History*) goes on to explain that when writing about history, empirically verifiable facts are of paramount importance and "interpretation" can often be highly misleading.

Immediately, Vinnie sets down her second quotation:

> 2. It's somewhat alarming for professional historians to consider the claim that the writing of history, at base, is no different from the writing of fiction. Those who make this claim seem to imply that we could even make a case for stating that Mr. Pickwick, who didn't exist but about whom we know a great deal, is more "real" than President Reagan, about whom we have a great number of "facts" but (at this stage) no coherent "story" which can't be undermined when we put the "facts" into a different pattern. We're forced to come to terms with this difficulty: historical "facts" are always mediated by an authorial consciousness.

Vinnie goes on the explain that Hal Wurijek, in his book, *Facts, Factoids, Tabloids and Tales*, from which this is taken, asserts that because facts are always perceived by an individual consciousness that makes a "pattern of significance," it's impossible when writing about history to avoid interpretation.

This opening move is very bold, but it feels right for Vinnie because she wants to show that the two views she's examining are, on the face of it, totally at odds. The silence between the two quotations is a transition which implies "Here's one idea, now here's its opposite." Having set them down, she finds a natural way to proceed by citing two more passages, one from Charles Dickens' *Pickwick Papers* and one from a recent biography of Ronald Reagan by Lou Cannon. Then she proceeds with her argument:

> Some things are clear from these two passages. What Dickens tells us about Mr. Pickwick is so full of lively detail that, as in all good fiction, it has the immediacy of "felt life." Mr. Pickwick is palpably "there" for us.

How to stop your papers from killing you (and me)

We could perhaps say, more accurately, Dickens writes *as if* he's there both for him and us. Those little words are crucially important. *As if* is the defining mode of fiction. We, the readers, know that Mr. Pickwick is an invention, yet we suspend our disbelief because we know that the art of reading about him is to pretend, with the author, that he really does exist. This is a contract that we make with open eyes though it is the job of a good author to make us, at least occasionally, forget the contract altogether.

The passage about President Reagan is much more problematical. We already know that Ronald Reagan, a sometime film-star, sometime Governor of California, was for eight years President of the United States. We therefore have an entirely different contract with this writer than we do with Charles Dickens. The paradox is that, although we get a great number of facts about this person, this account has little of the immediacy of the passage from Dickens, and we're left somehow disengaged, outside, detached. If this is the objectivity that Malmsby considers desirable in a historian's work, it raises problems. The writing is rather lifeless and in the long run tells us very little about this person who was president of the most powerful nation in the world. We're left with the unshakable and disturbing impression that the fiction of Dickens seems more convincing than the facts of the historian. A very odd conclusion.

Now, Vinnie needs a bridge-passage because her dialectic is about to take a different form. She has attended a recent symposium at the University of Chicago where her two authors deepen their discussion on the respective place of "fact" and "interpretation" in the writing of history. She takes a recording from that session, quotes some excerpts from it in her paper and shows that though Malmsby and Wurijek clarify their differences, they by no means resolve them. She then brings in another authority who seems to agree with Wurijek that no fact is an isolated thing, and when we write about history we are influenced very strongly by an overarching ideology which guides our selection of what "facts" we use. The author (Ambrose Langer, in *Facts and Their Limitations*) goes further. He intimates that because what we know of Ronald Reagan comes only from other people—who sometimes give very different views—and that Reagan was always an "actor" we will probably never know the final "facts" about him. Even more surprisingly, he suggests that in some ways he is less real than the fictional Mr. Pickwick, about whom we know great deal.

After a little more examination of this very difficult question, Vinnie is ready to make her conclusion:

> The chief question to ask here is whether the disagreement between Malmsby and Wurijek, and historians of their respective persuasion, is a disagreement about the nature of reality or about the nature and limits of knowledge. Wurijek would claim that our experience of anything—including that of so-called historical facts—is irredeemably subjective, partial, limited, and dynamic. There are no "final stories" and the only thing we can look for is an internal consistency in whatever pattern we find in, or impose on, the material. Historians rarely argue about whether Hitler was a house-painter, but they are always arguing about what, in the overall "pattern of significance," such an isolated piece of knowledge might mean.
>
> Malmsby would reply that it may well be that the fact of Hitler as a house-painter is relatively insignificant, but there are thousands of other facts about Hitler and his period which we should not either omit or distort in the name of some over-arching ideology when we're writing about that period. From where I stand now, something important is being said by both these authors. A history without facts is impossible to imagine. As Malmsby says, there is a real world and things happen in it and we try to record them. But a historian without an ideology and therefore, a temperament and a political bias to set his facts in motion (if we can imagine such a person) will probably give us such a poor beacon that he will illuminate very little. The problem that these two writers leave us with is whether there might be some way to reconcile their two opposing views. For the moment, the dilemma that they confront us with promises to remain with us for some time.

Note that Vinnie doesn't end her essay with a thesis. She rounds it off as best she can from the data she's been working with. The second thing to note is that although there's a good deal of quotation in her paper, Vinnie has kept complete charge of her argument. Finally, by using her authors as characters she has presented a lively dramatization of their ideas and of hers. It's useful to remind ourselves that the word *essay* comes from the French word *essayer*, which means "to try," or "try out." Good essays sometimes have the air of a scouting activity in which the idea of a definite conclusion is resisted because the facts can't be made to fit. In situations like this, as this essay shows, you have to keep the question open.

NINE:
Approaching Sideways

Since she first read it in high school, a short poem by James Wright has haunted Cheryl Pacey's imagination. Here's the complete text:

> **Autumn Begins In Martin's Ferry, Ohio**
> In the Shreve High football stadium,
> I think of Polacks nursing long beers in Tiltonsville,
> And grey faces of Negroes in the blast furnace at Benwood
> And the ruptured night watchman of Wheeling Steel,
> Dreaming of heroes.
>
> All the proud fathers are ashamed to go home.
> Their women cluck like starved pullets,
> Dying for love.
>
> Therefore,
> Their sons grow suicidally beautiful
> At the beginning of October,
> And gallop terribly against each other's bodies.

Cheryl didn't expect this to happen, but now she's found the chance to put her understanding of the poem to good use, not in a literature class but for a paper in Anthropology 8: Introduction to the Study of American Culture. Her task is to write on a subculture and how it relates to the context of the larger culture in which it occurs. The strategy she decides to use will appeal to those who like to make connections between things that are not normally related.

Cheryl has chosen American Football as her topic. She's had an extensive conversation with her teacher and explained that she would like to approach her essay by using Wright's poem as a springboard. Her teacher emphasized that anthropology is an inductive science in which the basic assertions have to be tested against the evidence. Cheryl explained that she intends to use the poem only as a way into her essay; it's not her central concern. Her teacher agreed tentatively with her plan and went on to point out some of the important subcultural elements she should consider. Then he urged her to get busy.

Cheryl does a lot of reading and after quoting Wright's poem continues with this:

> In a few lines Wright makes a disturbing criticism of one of our national "institutions." His argument is that football exists in this country because young men are driven to it through the thwarted dreams of their fathers. But there's a flip side to their dreams. According to Wright, the dreams become lethal—the wives/mothers are starving from emotional neglect and each spring the young men begin the yearly ritual of destroying themselves and each other.

Now she makes a short transition that states her intention go beyond the poem to examine the social structures that support the subculture of football. She will give a kind of expanded list beginning with the "military model" on which football is based, with the central paradox that football is a military game whose "foot-soldiers" (the players) are rewarded more highly than the "generals" (the coaches). This is because the military model is mediated by another cultural force that can be summed up in one word: Hollywood. Partly through the use of technology, such as slo-mo and freeze-frame, football players are transformed into stars. They become "culture heroes." A letter from the anthropologist R.T. Rosin to the author, while she is writing, reaffirms two important things: her paper in anthropology has to present solid evidence for her arguments and, second, it's not only the quarterback who can star in the game but almost any member of the team, so her "military model" needs to be qualified to include the idea that, though the Hollywood model cuts across it, the whole "military team" is not a hierarchy, but a peculiar kind of democracy.

Considering all these things Cheryl proceeds with her paper by closely examining the following factors in her chosen subculture:

—The function of schools and other institutions in reinforcing the subculture of football;

—The role of corporations and advertising, and the media;

—The function of newspapers and the constant presence of football on their pages;

—The cultural norm of manhood in which football has a major role.

Having elaborated on all these, Cheryl has made a first rough draft that she can let sit for a couple of days before she gives it close attention. She has considerable work to do but the essay is well on the way now, and in her next draft she will firm up her main ideas, which will allow her to work toward her thesis that she now drafts in very rough form:

> What I have tried to show here is that the game of football is a somewhat concentrated reflection of our most prominent national characteristics: our fascination with power and our respect for a kind of military precision, even in those activities we call our "games." I have mentioned only briefly three other things that I believe are equally important: our love of "success" and "winning," our sentimentality and our penchant for destruction, which seems to be a part of our physicality. All these things are often very closely related. It's common sight throughout the country—women, men and children huddled around a television watching the Big Game, all of them almost overwhelmed by emotion, the women yelling aggressively with the men, "Yeah, kill him" and hugging each other and weeping when "We" win. I would suggest

that it's no accident that both the violence and the sentimentality associated with football are of the same kind that we find in our culture at large and, it could be argued, in our foreign policy.

It will now be apparent why I have called this alternative form "approaching sideways." In using a poem as a way into an anthropological essay, Cheryl has made an interesting bridge between two fields which, conventionally, are thought to have little in common. This is an adventurous move but she has made her transition quite convincingly. In all this new thinking, Cheryl is showing that imaginative explorations are the living core of all good essays and it's clear that in writing this essay she's gaining confidence in developing her own skills. Many teachers find this kind of risk-taking, if it's handled well and produces thoughtful writing, highly commendable.

Let's turn now to something radically different.

TEN:
Prismatic Composition

This alternative, which has produced some highly provocative writing, might at first make you angry or frustrated. All I can ask is that you give it a fair reading and think about it. There are occasions when you might find it very useful.

Suppose you've just seen the play *Rosencrantz and Guildenstern Are Dead*, which you found very interesting, but difficult. You want to write about it but you can't at this point draw everything into a tight argument and thesis. There are too many puzzles. That thought may stop you in your tracks, but it needn't. In fact, here's where it can get very interesting. *You can make your whole essay a series of questions and speculations*. One way to begin is to focus intently on *one* thing in the play that really caught your imagination:

> When we watch *Hamlet* in the original we're aware of ourselves observing what happens in the fictional world of Elsinore Castle. In Tom Stoppard's play, *Rosencrantz and Guildenstern are Dead*, we watch the same characters—but everything's different. The play *Hamlet* has become the new "real" world and Rosencrantz and Guildenstern—instead of Hamlet, Claudius, Gertrude, Polonius and so on—are now the central characters. Yet they are more like anti-heroes than heroes. They haven't the least idea why they have been summoned by the King except for some vague notion that they have to humor Hamlet and, though they don't know this, to find out what's making him tick.

How to stop your papers from killing you (and me)

Jackson (the author of this draft) gives several instances in the play to make a general point about how central the idea of "playing" is in this work. His charge is to write a five-page paper in a course on Modern Experimental Theater. Having said all he wants to say about one kind of playing at this point, he decides to try an experiment on the essay form itself. So he types in an asterisk and comes at his topic from another angle.

*

In the opening scene of the play Rosencrantz and Guildenstern are having a kind of heated discussion about modern number theory. The audience finds it hard to follow and the speed of their dialogue doesn't make it any easier. I was reminded of some of the rapid-fire philosophical passages in Beckett's *Waiting for Godot* or Pinter's *The Homecoming* (get specific here). What Stoppard seems to be doing here and elsewhere in the play is showing us that if Hamlet, both the play and the character, are full of uncertainty, our own times are even more so. Nothing makes consistent sense. We have patches of jargon, snippets of information and number theory, punctuated with mystery and darkness. In this sense Stoppard's play is distinctly modern. He is playing with the play of Hamlet but his intentions are very serious. Paranoia is necessary in the world of Rosencrantz and Guildenstern as it seems to be in ours, and both Rosencrantz and Guildenstern have a good dose of it and, perhaps he is arguing, so should we.

Jackson makes another pause. Once again, he's done what some teachers of short fiction recommend: always stop too early. However, there's a lot more to say about this play. So he tries another tack.

*

On the ship going toward England Hamlet swaps the note written by Claudius, his new stepfather, and addressed to the King of England. It has been placed in the keeping of his two friends Rosencrantz and Guildenstern. That note asks the King to execute Hamlet. Hamlet steals the letter while his companions are sleeping, and he makes an emendation: he instructs the king to execute his companions, not himself. He then walks to the prow of the ship while they're sleeping on the deck and peers out into the audience. At this point we, the audience, have become a dark sea. Hamlet remains staring out at us for a long while and then his mouth forms a little ball of saliva and he spits, once, very softly out into the darkness, which is us. It's an astonishing moment, and I don't think I will ever understand what it means, and yet it seems entirely appropriate. Maybe it's associated with the fact that Rosencrantz and Guildenstern, who haven't done anything but obey orders, are nonetheless dispensable. They are a ball of saliva in Hamlet's mouth and they will dissolve into the sea. Or maybe Stoppard is saying we are all victims of political and other powers we don't understand. I don't know. But I do understand that that puzzle is in the play, and not just in my head. Or should I say it seems to be in the play?

This is enough to show the basic design of a prismatic essay. The idea is to take a subject and, just as one turns a prism to catch different facets in the light, you slowly revolve your topic and give different perspectives.

Considered as a response to an assignment, a problem obviously remains. Jackson may have opened up his topic in a way that seems challenging for both himself and his reader but he still needs to bring the segments of the prism to some kind of conclusion. If we look at the essay with this in mind we will see that there are three broad possibilities: he may wish to keep his conclusion very tentative because he is at this stage not at all confident about making one that draws the whole thing tight; second, he may feel he can bring everything to a *fairly* definite, but by no means definitive conclusion. Or, third, he may find he is able to make a conclusion in the form of a thesis statement. Here, in turn, are examples of those three possibilities:

I. TENTATIVE CONCLUSION

These five excursions into Stoppard's play are enough to show that the play opens up a number of puzzles which, at this stage of my own understanding, can't be definitively solved. It's clear that, as the title hints, Stoppard is, among other things, indulging in a kind of theatrical play. We could even say that he's playing with the idea of "play" itself.

That idea gets even more complex when we remember that a great deal of the original *Hamlet* is also about "playing." For very good reasons, Hamlet keeps his motives secret from all those around him. We might guess what they are but the "audience" in Elsinore Castle doesn't, and that's the way Hamlet wants it. He has to be secretive. Could we say the same about the Hamlet in Stoppard's play and extend the idea further and say that both Rosencrantz and Guildenstern are also in great danger? Could we extend that question even further and ask if Stoppard wants the audience to feel that they themselves are in also in peril? Stoppard is writing at a very different time from Shakespeare and, especially since the invention of the atom bomb and other highly destructive weapons and poisons, no one can call himself or herself safe. There's another question that I've pointed to. Could it be that Stoppard in his "playing" the numbers in the mathematical game (where the play begins) is asking this question: do we all live nowadays in a world which is not only largely unknown, but is perhaps unknowable? That's a much more troubling question and one which can probably be grappled with somewhat more satisfactorily if we look at Stoppard's work as a whole. That may be the best way to continue exploring.

2. MORE DEFINITE CONCLUSION

What I've tried to show here is that Stoppard is building a play on a foundation of another work of literature. This work can't be understood without some acquaintance with the original *Hamlet*. In other words, it's a very literary play and in some senses Stoppard is writing for those in the know. In this sense it could be called an "intellectual play" or a "play of ideas." The trouble is we are not quite sure what the ideas are. We can see that he's playing with modern mathematical notions and he's concerned in some sense with political intrigue but it's not at all clear what these concerns add up to. What I think we can say is this: Stoppard seems throughout to resist the idea of our finding a "solution" and certainly an overarching solution. So much of the dialogue, the characterization, and the sequencing of events leave us deeply puzzled. That doesn't seem to affect the overall theatrical brilliance of the play. Our attention is held throughout. Inferior plays quite often leave us with a sense of everything falling into place and we say "Oh, that's what it all meant." Not with this play. We see some things very clearly but we are not sure of their meaning. We come away slightly puzzled by some things, and very puzzled by the whole. Perhaps that's the real point.

3. CONCLUSION WITH A THESIS STATEMENT

My present finding from looking at these angles on the play is that Stoppard may have taken as his point of departure the very interesting study of Shakespeare by the Polish critic, Jan Kott, called *Shakespeare Our Contemporary*. Kott means by that title something very specific. His basic argument throughout the book is than in many of his plays Shakespeare is dealing with an Elizabethan world which is, politically, fraught with terrible danger. Kott's main point is that absolutely nothing has changed in that respect between Shakespeare's time and ours and, in fact, the situation has gotten worse. The world of espionage, secret prisons, international intrigues, betrayals, corruption and much more, is so widespread (Stoppard is arguing, after Kott) there is no hiding from it. Hamlet, in both plays, is caught in it like a fly in a spiderweb. He, in turn, entraps Rosencrantz and Guildenstern, who are innocent bystanders as far as the main action is concerned. They have no idea why they are involved, and they die unenlightened. The world gives no more "conclusions" than the game of numbers they are playing. That applies to all of us. There is no "script," no "fate," no "destiny"—or none that any of us can know about. Things happen, and they sometimes have a very dark side, such as they do both in *Hamlet* and in Stoppard's variation on that play. What his work leaves us with is a sense of foreboding. Fortunately, that sense is held in check by the fact that the play, as theater and drama, is very "enjoyable." To bring those two seemingly contradictory things together is an intellectual and dramatic feat of the first order.

*

Some will object that the more "open" forms of prismatic composition do not satisfy the requirements of a proper academic essay. I think this is a narrow view. Some problems are obdurately difficult and cannot, in all honesty, be forced toward a conclusion. They need, instead, to be opened up and explored.

It goes without saying that you should use Prismatic Composition very judiciously and only after adequate consultation with your teacher. It's not suitable for all essays, or even most, but is particularly useful for delving into something you find imaginatively resistant.

ELEVEN:
Mixed Forms

As you think in depth about the nature of your topic and the questions you might want to explore, structural ideas which you wouldn't normally consider within a conventional essay may occur to you. For instance, had she more time to develop a much longer paper, Cheryl Pacey's essay on football could have included such things as excerpts from a locker-room meeting, interviews with a number of players, diagrams of an offensive play, excerpts from speeches, or quotations from scholars of game-theory, and so on. The idea is to choose those sources which best illustrate the major points you're trying to make.

The way you create an essay of mixed forms will depend on the nature of the subject matter and on your own temperament. One size does not fit all. Vinnie's essay, which I classified as an example of dialectical composition, is also an essay of mixed forms. She uses significant quotations and dialogue and both these elements are framed by an analytical commentary of her own. Although she uses a number of other voices as characters in her narrative of ideas, the essay is very much her own. That's important in everything you write, no matter what form you choose: you essay is *your intellectual home*. It must feel right for you.

In thinking about mixed forms you should let your imagination range. If, for instance, you want to examine a question in educational psychology and its implications for the way we devise our curricula in primary schools, you may want to include opinions and quotations from some, or all of the following:

>A school superintendent
>
>Two opposing religious authorities
>
>A newspaper article
>
>Letters to the editor
>
>Academic psychologists
>
>Parents
>
>Plato's ideas on education
>
>Interviews with children

and/or much else. The final design will be something that you find not only responsible in substance but aesthetically pleasing.

All these alternatives, as well as others you might invent yourself, can be very rewarding. At first you will find it difficult to leave the old comfortable habits behind, but as you go more deeply into your subject matter and think more about the *arrangement* you're making to encompass it, this concentration on the *writing* becomes a totally new way of looking at your essays.

Although this little inventory of alternative forms is by no means exhaustive it will, perhaps, give you some new possibilities to think about.

So far we have had an overall view of six possible essay-forms. Now I want to zoom in for a closer look at several matters which we must wrestle with no matter what form of the essay we choose.

PART IV
TWO KEYS TO EFFECTIVE NARRATION

TWELVE:
Quotations as Characters

Quotations in your essays are not a substitute for your own voice; they are other people's voices which help you reveal your own argument. In this sense they're like characters in a play or a story. That has to be emphasized very strongly because in some sectors of academia the following kind of quotation is believed to be entirely in order. (The author's own words are in bold type):

>**Attempts to promote a universal health-scheme in this country** "have been vigorously opposed since the period of the New Deal by a great number of institutions and political lobbyists."[1] **Among these are**, "all those organizations who bridle at the very idea of what they call 'government medicine', the A.M.A. who sees its hegemony threatened, and even millions of ordinary citizens who have been taught to distrust big government and 'creeping socialism.'"[2] **The result is that** "the U.S. lags considerably behind several other countries— notably Germany, Canada and Sweden—in the provision of adequate medical care for millions of its citizens."[3]

I would argue that this kind of quotation is entirely unacceptable because the so-called "author" has all but disappeared. He has merely hijacked someone else's words so that they form a kind of loose continuity with his own. Admittedly, there's no attempt to deceive; everything is properly footnoted. Yet, it's as if the author is saying: "I can't write very well, but I've found an authority who can do it for me." An essay written in this way is inauthentic. As with the earlier essay on Hamlet, there is no one at home, and absent authors can say nothing worth reading.

If part of your training has been to quote in this manner, there are two ways to get beyond it. The first is fairly simple. Here's an example:

> Throughout his whole writing career, Eliot was accused of all kinds of unacceptable literary behavior. After he had written *The Waste Land* various critics claimed that he was nothing but "an anthologizer, a pasticheur"[1] whose main occupation seemed to be to string together the great lines of earlier poets in a way which made little sense. W.B. Yeats went so far as to say he was "more of a critic than a poet"[2] and one wonders whether Yeats' critique sprang from the threat of Eliot's fame. Eliot's own sense of his poem is a little hard to fathom. At one time he called it "a wholly insignificant grouse against life,"[3] but at other times he seemed to set great store by it. As with the poem itself, we are faced with a puzzling problem. How, given these very different notions from the author, and others, should we read *The Waste Land*?

We might call these embedded quotations. They are clearly nothing like those in the first example because here the author is thoroughly present in her prose. Though the embedded quotations are quite distinct from her own voice she uses them to develop her own argument—which in this case is a question. A more advanced example can be found in the following excerpt from a draft essay by Priscilla Mandl on Leonardo da Vinci's knot diagrams:

> Leonardo's notebooks are filled with sketches of whorls and waterswirls and circulating forms. Many artists have made such sketches. What's unusual about da Vinci's examples is that they are precisely drawn, rather complex knot-forms, all arranged in geometric patterns. Engerstrom, in discussing these figures in his earliest book on da Vinci, says this:
>> The knot-forms are at first puzzling because they seem only intricate two-dimensional designs and are quite separate from the water-forms, which belong to his "studies in nature."

Then we realize that we're looking at them the wrong way. They are three-dimensional forms, sometimes in the shape of cones, with their apexes "nearer" the observer's eye. Much more important, we remember that da Vinci all his life was a troubled person and the knots clearly have a psychological dimension. He was interested in, one might say obsessed, by the fact that a knot ("noue" in French) has to be "recognized" so that a dé-noue-ment (un-knotting) can take place. First, then, you have to see the "knot" very clearly. In other words, these manifold "knot" patterns are, for da Vinci, not a form of visual doodling but the outward sign of a serious inner exercise.[1]

This observation sounds very interesting but it's not as convincing as it seems. As many people have pointed out, very little has been verified concerning da Vinci's neuroses (1,2,3). There are no detailed marginal commentaries on the notebook pages that contain the knots, as there are on hundreds of others of his sketches and diagrams. Finally, the kinds of knot mandalas that da Vinci creates aren't found in any other artist of the period and, as far as I have been able to discover, there is no widely accepted knot symbolism in Renaissance art. Engerstrom's remarks therefore raise more questions than they answer. Leonardo's knot-forms remain puzzling and we have to look elsewhere for an explanation...

In this example the author stays at all times in charge of her main argument. She uses the quotation from Engerstrom as a way of marshalling her own ideas, which are very different from his. The quotation, in other words, becomes a new voice in the essay—one which furthers her own analysis. Priscilla is the chief protagonist. The quotation from Engerstrom is an antagonist. These two provide the tension which allows this part of her essay to develop.

Some essays are a whole orchestra of different voices. Vinnie's essay on Fiction and History contains the voices of two historians—in written form, and as a transcript from a tape—as well as Mr. Pickwick, and President

Reagan's biographer: five voices, all held in balance by the central voice of the author.

The important thing to remember is to use quotations *only* when they help you. When you dramatize your ideas using different "characters" it can be very satisfying. It makes the ideas in your essay—yours and those of your sources—much more vivid and memorable.

That brings us to the last, and possibly the most difficult of our keys to the effective development of your argument.

THIRTEEN:
Mastering Transitions

No essay is merely a collection of facts and ideas. It's an intellectual exploration where those two things are linked together into a coherent and developing pattern. That's why most writers spend a good deal of time wrestling with their transitions. When stuck, they have to ask: *exactly how are these ideas related?*—and they have to get a clear answer before they can continue. With that in mind, let's look closely at an example from an essay we've already encountered. You'll recall that Lance concluded his opening paragraph on Japanese Temple-Gardens with this sentence:

> There are some old men, who appear to be monks, sitting quietly in the courtyard.

He begins his next paragraph with this:

> My curiosity was aroused by what I saw. Why such a dry, formal garden, and what was the relation between the garden and the monastery?

This works because Lance twigged instinctively something so simple that it's easy to miss. He realized that *each sentence must have two eyes.* That sounds odd, I know, so I'll explain what I mean. If a sentence is part of a narrative continuity, in order to prevent it being an isolate, *it has to look back at what's already been said as well as to anticipate what's coming.* As Lance's sentence is a transition between two paragraphs, not only two sentences, it also has to glance over its shoulder at the whole last paragraph, and look forward to the next one.

To be specific: in his first paragraph Lance had given a detailed description of the temple and the garden, so his transition sentence can be unpacked to mean something like this: "My curiosity was aroused by all that I saw (in the scene I have just outlined in the previous paragraph.)" The transition sentence can likewise be read in this way: "I will now explain, in my next paragraph, why my curiosity was aroused." This might seem a tedious explanation of an apparently simple connection. But Lance's sentence is not nearly as simple as it seems. It's part of a sequence which gathers the previous material, then, as it were, throws it forward in anticipation of what will follow.

Lance, at this point, is providing a straightforward narrative account of what he saw. Difficulties arise when we move from a description of objects and events to argument. In this latter kind of transition, which is much more common in an academic paper, the two eyes in each sentence have to see the *logical* relation between your ideas. We can't make firm transitions between one sentence and the next, nor between one paragraph and the next unless the two eyes are both working properly to make that logical pattern firm.

Consider this case from Vinnie's essay on Fiction and History:

> ...To go back to our two protagonists: both Malmsby and Wurijek would agree that there was a person called Ronald Reagan living in America at a certain definable period in time. Mr. Pickwick, on the other hand, is a product of Charles Dickens's imagination, and he therefore exists in quite a different realm. They would also agree that we cannot have a true history of Mr. Pickwick which will tell us the real facts about him. Dickens has already provided us with all the evidence we're going to get. Ronald Reagan is a much more open project. More and more evidence about him can accrue, at least theoretically, until the end of time.
>
> **These** two people are therefore utterly different data. So much is clear. The trouble arises **here**: all that most of us know about Ronald Reagan is what we have read about him, or seen in various kinds of film—documentary, or otherwise. Many of us have seen some of this evidence

first-hand. But we have to take account of the possible fact that Reagan was always and everywhere an actor. We know other facts: his assistant Bruce Deaver was with him very early on many mornings during his occupancy of the White House and often handed him the script for the presidential role he would play that day, and helped him rehearse it...

The two eyes in the transition are the words marked in bold type: **These** and **here**. **These** looks back to the double subject of the last paragraph, Ronald Reagan and Mr. Pickwick. The second eye, **here**, looks forward to what will follow in this new paragraph. It's a very powerful pointer because it anticipates a paradox: in one sense, President Reagan and Mr. Pickwick are "utterly different data" but, as the paragraph develops, we realize that, in another way, they are somewhat similar. This logical connection could not have been made clear if the eyes had been weak. The process of surveying what's been said, then looking forward has been effectively performed because the paradoxical relation between the ideas has been accurately perceived, then stated.

When you're stuck with a transition, think about the exact relation between the two ideas you're struggling with, then check to see that each sentence has two eyes—it will help the sense of continuity you're looking for.

It may be useful here to make a very brief inventory of some of the typical kinds of relations one finds between ideas, and the kind of transitions they entail.

You may want your transition to *modify* what you have already said, in which case, you might write something like one of these:

> That gives a slightly inaccurate picture because...
> As this is based on a partial reading. I must now...
> I have been speaking so far as if there were only one kind of empathy but, in fact, there are several...

or to *amplify* significantly what you have already said. In which case you might use:

> This is only a sketch of the problem and the details need to be filled out...
> Admittedly, these are both very important causes but the really important one is somewhat more elusive...
> Einstein went on from such early calculations to something so radical that it changed the whole course of physics...

or to *contradict* what you have already said with something like one of these:

> Although that claim sounds very plausible, at least three modern philosophers have shown it is based on faulty reasoning...
> That was the earlier assumption. Then came quantum mechanics, turning the old physics on its head...
> Blake said the exact opposite. He claimed that we see not *with* but *through* the eye...

or to *disagree in part* with what you've already said with:

> This notion has much to be said for it, but we must look at its implications more closely...
> The statement holds true only in certain cases...
> If we exclude Greenland, that analysis has a certain merit but...

These are only some of the very many ways of signaling how the ideas in one sentence or paragraph can relate to those in the sentence or paragraph that will follow. Such signaling of exact relations is one of the chief skills that writers call on. Forging accurate transitions is often a question of trial and error and it requires a good deal of attention.

Here are some transitions I've jotted down from my own recent reading. When you're stuck and can't find the right link you may want to look at the types of transition I've given above, and at the following list. They may help you move forward:

> Whatever the reasons, these pre-historic communities manufactured a unique kind of pottery that...
> Similar findings were published by the Royal Society in...
> Most politicians have no quarrel with that, but one maverick senator does...
> In short, in spite of all his so-called "daydreaming," Bainbridge had a very practical imagination, which is shown in his...
> Let's put all that in another way...
> Worse yet, the problem is not only the military losses but...
> When we take all this into account, it makes only minimal sense for this reason: ...
> This resembles an ending devised by a novelist; an economist would give an entirely different account...
> And what of Hemingway himself at this time?...
> What Kray discovered in those experiments was it was not the size of the organelle that mattered but...
> He knew that somewhere in all this welter of information there had to be a pattern which revealed...
> While biographers of this kind emphasize "facts," others have a different approach...
> Yet there was nothing to find; all the research revealed that...

Clearly, there are many more, but these few may serve as prompts to get you thinking about the variety of possible relations between your ideas which, in your advanced drafts, you will need to make clear to yourself and your reader.

Second Interlude

The Uses of Précis-Writing

If free-writing, which I discussed in the *First Interlude,* can be seen as the Art of Letting Go, the art of précis writing is, in a sense, its opposite. In free-writing you go into a kind of *reverie* and try out all kinds of imaginative possibilities to arrive at a rough draft of what you want to say. Précis writing requires a different mental stance: you have to stand back and be fully *conscious* of what's being said so that you can begin to pare it down to essentials.

The skills you learn in précis-writing will give you an invaluable tool to use in all aspects of rewriting and editing. It teaches you how to delete unnecessary words, phrases, sentences and paragraphs. It forces you to ask the question: *what am I really driving at in this sentence, paragraph—or my essay as a whole?* When you can answer that question your writing will gain strength and clarity.

The best way to practice précis writing is to take a passage of someone else's prose and reduce it to its essential meaning. There are a number of strategies which will help you here. Let's take a particular example and see how they apply. Here's the first draft of the beginning of an essay on Price Dynamics in the Stock Market:

> The up and down behavior of the stock market is a reaction to an enormous variety of factors, many of which are possibly beyond our present understanding. One overall explanation that's often been put forward to try to bring that behavior into an understandable framework is called the theory of the "Efficient Market." Its basic assumption is that the market responds very precisely to all the various forces and factors operating on it at any one time. This theory, which is held quite tenaciously by many financial theorists, has a major logical shortcoming. (94 words)

Even on first reading you'll sense how that can be improved. For a start, too many words are being used to express relatively simple ideas. That happens in nearly all first drafts, and it's nothing to be concerned about. In later drafts, however, the task is to take out what linguists call the "noise"—the words that do not contribute to the meaning. But how do you decide which words are noise? The answer is by careful reading of what's being said, by intuition, and by trial and error. Let's look again at the first sentence:

The basic meaning of *The up and down behavior of the stock market*, etc. can be expressed much more economically. Either *Stock market fluctuations* or *Fluctuations in the stock market* will suffice. Likewise with the rest of the sentence. You might try out several possibilities and arrive, tentatively, at this:

> Stock market fluctuations have a multiplicity of causes, many of which are presently obscure.

which uses a little over half the words of the original.

If you continue editing down to the essentials in this way you might get something like this:

> One common explanation for these fluctuations is called the Efficient Market Theory, **whose** central assumption is that markets respond very precisely to all the factors operating on them at any one time. This theory, though tenaciously held by many economists, is deeply flawed. (again, a considerable reduction from 68 to 43 words)

Note that two sentences in the first draft have been linked together by the word *whose* and the new version also sounds much more natural.

When we put all this together we have a first paragraph which reads this way:

> Stock market fluctuations have a multiplicity of causes, many of which are presently unknown. One common explanation for these fluctuations is called the Efficient Market Theory, whose central assump-

tion is that the market responds very precisely to all the factors operating on it at any one time. This theory, though tenaciously held by many economists, is deeply flawed. (58 words)

The 94 words of the first draft have been reduced to 58, but that's not the only criterion for effective editing. By cutting taking away all the surrounding fuzz, and by judicious linking, the essential ideas have been made clearer. Several important things have to be noted here. When you cut down drastically you can sometimes make your prose sound like a slightly expanded telegram. You don't want that. Your final copy should sound as natural as clear speech.

Second, good editing is much more than a mechanical *reduction*. Sometimes, as you edit down, you will find it very useful to *rearrange* your ideas so they knit together more firmly. Here's an example from the same essay:

> The efficient market theory, to have any value, has to apply to all markets. And it has to account for all the factors which influence market prices. What it failed to consider in this case, as in many others, was that some of the causes of market dynamics lie outside "pure" economics. The Greek market fall, like others, was driven by a panic, which feeds on itself and which is not quantifiable...

Here, an essential distinction between economic factors and psychological factors is not made clearly enough, and as that distinction is very important in the whole argument some rearranging is necessary:

> The "efficient market" theory considers only the "economic factors" which cause the market to behave as it does. What the theory does not and cannot take into account is that market movements are to a considerable extent driven by forces outside the realm of "pure" economics. In the Greek, and many other markets, fear and even outright panic drove the market. These psychological forces feed on themselves and are unquantifiable.

In all précis-writing your overall aim is concision. However, as I've shown in the above case, sometimes it is necessary to reorder the original ideas to make them clearer and, *very occasionally*, for the sake of precision, you may have to *add* something. As long as you keep in mind the idea that the *basic* aim is to edit down, a little rearrangement or amplification won't interfere with that aim.

It may be useful to set down a brief checklist of précis-writing strategies:

—Take out all the words that get in the road of your meaning. When in doubt be **over-bold**. If your surgery has been too severe your idea will cry out to be restored, perhaps in a shortened form. The old maxim "When in doubt, leave it out" really works. It reveals immediately what can't be dispensed with.

—Where you have a *group* of examples you can sometimes bring them together under one heading. In the essay we were just examining the first draft contains this:

> We simply do not have a mechanism for separating out the "pure" economic factors from all the rest. Yet these "outside" factors can have a profound and sometimes lasting effect on the economy taken as a whole. Workers are laid off, industries fail, people cannot afford food, houses cannot be sold, or bought, credit ratings are downgraded and the whole thing evolves into a descending spiral of misfortune which can, and sometimes does, spin out of control.

This paragraph is an obvious candidate for editing down, to something like this:

> There is presently no mechanism for separating out the "pure" economic factors from the rest. Yet these "outside" factors can have a profound and enduring effect on **all aspects of the economy**. Fear can lead to a descending spiral of mis-

fortune which, as in the Great Depression of 1929, can spin out of control.

Here, particulars in the original: *Workers are laid off, industries fail, people cannot afford food,* are all brought together under the more general *all aspects of the economy.* In losing these particulars the writing may be weakened; that point needs careful attention. In any kind of editing where your overall aim is to shorten you have to balance that aim against the desire to make your prose rich and colorful. Each decision will depend on the *degree* of shortening that's required.

—Often, when a first draft is too wordy it's because a main idea has been repeated in a slightly different way. If you examine your prose and find that this has occurred, edit down with the aim of stating that idea *once only*, as clearly as you can.

—The last, and most important thing is this: You must strike to the essential meaning and be able to state it succinctly. If you can't do that you can't move on. If you can, you can.

The art of précis-writing is really a form of courtesy to your reader and to yourself. It teaches you to be concise. Particularly now, in a climate of half-truths and unfounded pronouncements we owe it to each other to speak and write clearly.

If you've had little exposure to précis-writing you might find the exercises below a useful introduction. In these exercises try not to reinterpret and rewrite the author's ideas in a different way. Stay as close as you can to what you believe are *their* ideas and emphases.

1. REDUCE TO 80 WORDS

There was something about the man, that was all there was to it. He was six feet tall and very slender, and had on a trench coat and a porkpie hat, which he wore at a rakish angle, so that people, women in particular, could not help taking notice. His face had a refined quality. With closely cropped black curls framing high cheekbones and startling blue eyes that radiated a strange intensity. He stuck out in Santa Fe like a sore thumb. But it was not his unusual looks, his city clothes, or even the pipe that he waved about in one hand while talking that caught Dorothy McGibbin's attention. It was something in his bearing, the way he walked on the balls of his feet, which "gave the impression he was hardly touching the ground."

Jennet Conant: *109 East Palace*, New York, Simon & Schuster, p. 1

(135 words)

2. REDUCE TO 100 WORDS

Traditionally in Europe, oil-pressing was a cottage industry. Villages and towns had their own small oil press. Oil presses required parts that could withstand several tons of pressure per square inch, and they were difficult to clean and maintain; therefore they were (and are) too costly and complex for every home to have and maintain. Many older people who lived in Europe before the Second World War remember how fresh oils were sold door to door like milk and eggs. Fresh flax oil was delivered once a week in small ml. transparent glass bottles. Since oil was unprotected from light and air, it lasted only a few days. Research showing the importance of protecting oils from destruction by light, oxygen, and heat had not yet been done, but people knew from experience that the best oils turn rancid quickly and then taste bad, so they had to be bought in small quantities before they spoiled, just like fresh vegetables, milk, and eggs. Like fresh produce, unrefined oil was a staple in many homes.

Udo Erasmus: *Fats that Heal, Fats that Kill,* p. 174.

(185 words)

3. Reduce to 85 words

If biology is destiny, as Freud told us, what becomes of free will? It is tempting to think that deep within the brain lives a soul, a free agent that takes account of the body's experience but travels around the cranium of its own accord, reflecting, planning, and pulling the levers of the neuromotor machinery. The great paradox of determinism and free will, which has held the attention of the wisest philosophers and psychologists for generations, can be phrased in more biological terms as follows: if our genes are inherited and our environment is a train of physical events set in motion before we were born, how can there be a truly independent agent in the brain? The agent itself is created by the interaction of the genes and the environment. It would appear that freedom is only a self-delusion.

E.O. Wilson: *On Human Nature*. Cambridge, Mass. 1978, p. 71

(139 words)

*

If you are new to précis-writing, take these exercises slowly. If you can reduce them to the stipulated word-length and preserve the intended meaning without too much difficulty you are well on the way to being a competent editor of your own work.

PART V
FINE-TUNING: WHERE THE ANGELS LIVE

FOURTEEN:
Pointers for Editing

If you think you can compete your essay in one draft you're either deluding yourself or you're a true genius, in which latter case you wouldn't need to read this book. Most essay-writers, even professionals, have to take their work through at least four drafts. They're not totally separate drafts, of course. It might be better to call them stages, or levels of intensity, which increase in their attention to detail as they approach the final draft. The analytic skills you develop in précis-writing are very useful in all but the first of these stages. The last three stages—rewriting and editing, giving final form to your thesis or conclusion, and finding a suitable title—are all governed by the same principles. We could describe the whole process something like this: First, the free-writing of a rough draft, written quickly, without too much attention to small details. This draft is bound to have redundancies and awkwardly expressed ideas, and even material that later you will want to throw out entirely. The second stage is where you look over all your rough notes and ask yourself, "What am I getting at in this paper?" Only when you can give a clear answer to that question are you ready to proceed to your third draft where you begin to cut out everything inessential.

The third draft is usually the place where all the major editing and rearranging takes place. You check your footnotes, phrasing and sentence-structure, you look up words about which you have even the slightest uncertainty, you test the logic of your arguments. You also read your essay aloud, listening for anything that sounds wrong. You excise wordy passages and expand on things you've skimped. When you've completed all that you may think you are at the end, but you will nearly always be mistaken, because if you leave your "final" draft sit for a few days you'll discover a host of little things that need finer tuning. For instance, in the early draft of an essay on the Iran-Contra Affair, Jill Esposito was reasonably pleased with this passage:

> North was like a soldier who had been wronged while trying to be loyal to his ultimate commander, President Reagan. Poindexter seemed more like a bureaucrat. You could hear the computer clicking behind his words as he answered questions from the Senators. Many times that answer was "I can't recall." These two witnesses, though they appeared separately, seemed like a team. As the hearing developed a strange story emerged—a story in which William Casey was intimately involved. Casey was now dead but his presence seemed to be there in the Senate Chamber...

When she looked it over next day she realized with a few changes she could make it much stronger:

> North was like a soldier who, in trying to show his loyalty to his hidden commander, President Reagan, intimated that even by being called to appear before the Senatorial committee, he had been deeply wronged. His testimony was by turns aggressive, petulant and self-serving. Poindexter, by contrast, seemed more like a dry bureaucrat. You could hear the click of a computer behind his words as he answered questions from the Senators. Many times that answer was "I can't recall." In spite of their differences, these two witnesses seemed like a team and, together, they wove a strange story. Over that story hovered the powerful ghost of William Casey who, fortunately for both North and Poindexter, was now dead.

Several things stand out immediately. Consider the two versions of her final sentence:

Casey was now dead but his presence seemed to be there in the Senate Chamber.

Over that story hovered the powerful ghost of William Casey who, fortunately for both North and Poindexter, was now dead.

There are several reasons why the second one tells a better story. By splitting her main clause and interposing the words, *fortunately for both North and Poindexter*, she has made Casey much more defunct because her sentence now ends on the key word *dead*. The rhythm is also surer. The sentence doesn't just give the facts. It slows down at the end with two strong beats (**now** / **dead**). *By doing that she makes her sentence enact its meaning.* But she has done more: she has added the word *powerful* to characterize the ghost of Casey, and that ghost *hovers* over the hearings. These are small changes but they are very significant because she has transformed her original ordinary prose into something vivid and memorable.

We could put it this way: in her final draft Jill is interested in the art of **writing**, not just the "subject matter." She has listened carefully to her rhythm, tempo, variation of sentence-shape, and much more. When you're doubtful about your own writing you should read it aloud and ask yourself: *does the sound and rhythm of my prose reveal my meaning, or obscure it?* Even for professional writers, words, sentences and paragraphs are tricky things. A tiny change in tone, rhythm or emphasis, or a different word order, can radically transform a sentence, a paragraph—or even a whole essay.

*

Finally, an old bugbear for those who have difficulty arriving at the right length for their papers:

Suppose when she had finished what she thought was her final draft of the Oppenheimer essay Jan discovered that it was three pages too long. She had to cut it down without damaging the whole and she would need a sensible plan, not just an arbitrary counting of words. Her first task will be an overall paring, using what she has learned from her practice in précis-writing. She needs to home in on the *substance* of her essay and make sure every word that's not earning its place is jettisoned.

If that's not enough, she has to get more particular. You'll remember she examined four major points concerning Oppenheimer's career:

—his work as a scientist and leader of the Manhattan Project;

—the long and rather equivocal association he had with the Communist Party;

—the conflict with Edward Teller;

—Lewis Strauss and the legal Hearing that brought Oppenheimer down.

She needs to weigh, once again, the importance of each of these in her essay as a whole. If only one seems overlong she will have to work at cutting it back. Maybe she will need to shorten all four. If she finds that still doesn't suffice she may have to do something more drastic: she may have to leave out one of the major points altogether, or mention it only briefly. What's required in a case like this is to reconsider the design *and* the size of your essay as a whole. This is the kind of editing task that professional writers face nearly every day. They look for the main points, and when they have to, cut back appropriately.

Now let's take the opposite contingency: Suppose Jan discovers that her paper is three pages *short*. Her first reaction might be: *I will have to pad*. But she knows that if she does that it will lead to flabby repetition which would be boring for her and annoying for her readers. *It will always show.*

When faced with this contingency there's a much better alternative. You look over your whole essay again to see if one or all of your main ideas can be profitably developed a little further. For instance, you might be able to find an authority who either agrees or disagrees with you on a specific point and use that authority in the way I discussed in the chapter on quotations.

If your "final" draft is *very considerably* short of the required length and none of the above will suffice you may have to think about adding *another* important point to strengthen your overall thesis. In Jan's case, in considering all the things that molded Oppenheimer's fate, she may now include a substantial point about how Oppenheimer's brother and his circle of friends, who had close affiliations with the Communist Party, had contributed to his "guilt by association."

In sum, if your draft is either too long or too short there's a solution to hand. What's needed is situational intelligence, and each of your essays is a different situation. In either case—too long, or too short—a reconsideration of what you are aiming at in your essay *as a whole* will usually point you, quite quickly, in the right direction.

FIFTEEN:
Honing Your Conclusion, Finding a Title

Your conclusion is arguably the most important part of the your essay because it sums up the contribution you're making. For this reason, in most cases the early draft of your conclusion will nearly always need considerable revision.

Conclusions usually take one of three broad forms, as I pointed out in the chapter on Prismatic Composition. You can bring everything together into a firm thesis statement; you can propose a *tentative* thesis which needs further exploration; or you can show that all that you've examined so far leads to a challenging question or problem which can't at this stage be resolved, or not, at any rate, by you.

Let's look at the first and third possibilities a little more closely. Here's what Cheryl first wrote to conclude her essay on the subculture of football:

> What I have tried to show here is that the game of football is a somewhat concentrated reflection of our most prominent national characteristics: our fascination with power and our respect for a kind of military precision, even in those activities we call our "games." I've mentioned briefly three other things that I believe are equally important: our love of "success" and "winning," our sentimentality, and our penchant for destruction, which seems to be a part of our physicality. All these things are often very closely related. It's common sight throughout the country—women, men and children huddled around a television watching the Big Game, all of them almost overwhelmed by emotion, the women

yelling aggressively with the men, "Yeah, kill him" and hugging each other and weeping when "We" win. I would suggest that it's no accident that both the violence and the sentimentality associated with football are of the same kind that we find throughout the history of Hollywood and, it could be argued, in our foreign policy.

Even as she wrote that Cheryl knew it would only be a sketch. It was too verbose and informal and, in the wrong way, too "personal." For example, her dislike of people—especially women—gathering around the television and giving raucous advice to the players had deflected her from her main argument. Much of what she had written in this early conclusion had to be recast. The whole thing needed to be "cooler," more succinct and more in keeping with the requirements of academic writing. So now she takes this original conclusion through several more drafts and arrives at what she considers something more satisfactory:

> ...In other words, the game of football in our culture has become domesticated and normalized. It's for this reason that the dynamic process between the subculture of football and society as a whole can be seen as that of a complex, slightly distorted mirroring in which the values of the one reflect those of the other, and the integrity of both are thereby reinforced. In the game of football we have found a safe public way of revealing our aggressiveness as well as our strengths, both of which can perhaps be related to our political beliefs and our policies concerning our adversaries, and potential adversaries in the rest of the world.

That's much better, and much shorter. She knows there's still something wrong with the last sentence but she's almost there.

Vinnie, having completed her draft-essay Fiction and History, asked herself: "What have I discovered in all this?" and she tried to respond as honestly as she could:

From where I stand now, something important is being said by both these authors. A history without facts is impossible to imagine. As Malmsby says, there is a real world and things happen in it and we try to record them. But a historian without an ideology, without, therefore a temperament, and a political bias to set his facts in motion (if we can imagine such a person) will probably give us such a poor beacon that it will illuminate very little. The problem that these two writers leave us with is whether there might be some way to reconcile their two opposing views. For the moment, the dilemma that they confront us with promises to remain with us for some time.

She may have wanted to give a more definite conclusion in the form of a thesis statement but, at this stage, she couldn't. So she did what she had to do: she wrote honestly about her incomplete findings.

*

Even professional writers sometimes find titling their work very difficult. They know their title has to reveal something about the work in hand and at the same time it has to arouse their reader's curiosity. One very useful way of thinking about a title is to see it as a kind of radical précis of your thesis. Let's take a couple of examples from draft-essays we've already looked at to show what I mean.

In Rick's "false thesis" paper on the poem of Robert Frost the title he gave on what he thought was his final draft was *That Other Road: Study of a Poem by Robert Frost*. Just before he handed the essay in Rick realized that it didn't really point to the topic of his paper, which was, as you recall, that the usual interpretation of *The Road Not Taken* isn't supported by a close reading of the text. So he thought hard and came up with what he felt was something better: *That Other Meaning: A Reading of Frost's The Road Not Taken*.

This was an improvement but it still didn't capture what he was driving at. Then, while brewing coffee, he had a flash. This often happens when, after much concentration, you turn to a more casual task. In any case, suddenly Rick's title was there. *The Meaning Not Taken: Study of a Poem by Robert Frost*. He believed this was a distinct improvement because everyone's familiar with the title of the Frost poem, which Rick slyly echoes. Not only that, Rick's whole approach is somewhat playful and this new title gives a foretaste of that. Now his title is an integral part of the essay, not just something loosely tacked on—a small but really significant change.

Cheryl Pacey had to struggle harder for her title. She had originally written: *A Complex Mirror: Football and American Culture*. That was okay, but she wanted something more accurate, and more inviting for the reader. Knowing that the seeds of a suitable title can often be found at the end of an essay, she looks over her last paragraph:

> In other words, the game of football in our culture, etc

What had interested her throughout was a reciprocal *process*—the function of football in American society as a whole. She is trying to say they are intimately related *but not in a one-to-one manner*. She jots down two possibilities:

A Distorted Mirror: Football in American Culture

A Distorting Mirror: Football, etc

Because they both conjure up the mirrors one sees at fun-fairs she crosses them out and tries another possibility:

A Distilling Mirror; Football, etc

That won't work either. Mirrors don't distill. Then she sees something else. The relation between the two things is not static. She wants to convey the idea of a *dynamic*, reciprocal process which she'd pointed to in the word *mirroring*.

So she jots down:

Football and American Culture: A Mirroring

That's closer, but it's a little bland.

Several hours later she tries again:

An Inexact Mirroring: Football, etc

This, she senses, is much closer. The new word still works well because she's turned the static noun *mirror* into the its active gerund, *mirroring*. It's a tiny change but significant. Then, just before she goes to bed, she realizes the word *Inexact* is a poor choice because what she's saying is that the relation between the two things—football and culture—is not only a dynamic process, but one that's also surprising and even, in certain respects, upside down. (She's thinking particularly of the point she made about the "foot-soldiers" being, in one sense, superior to the "generals.")

She continues with her trial-and-error process, hoping to find something that will both inform and interest her reader. Her deliberations lead to something quite simple. Next morning, she looks over all the possibilities and comes up with these two final candidates:

A Complex, Inexact Mirroring: Football in American Culture

A Paradoxical Mirroring: Football in American Culture

Both are better than any of the earlier versions; the new word *paradoxical* is almost exactly what she wants because it contains the notions of complexity, surprise and inexactitude. She sleeps on it and, on waking, decides firmly on the second choice. At the head of her essay she types in the new title, with a slight (and final) change:

A Paradoxical *Mirroring*: Football and *American* Culture

Now she's ready to print the whole thing.

SIXTEEN:
Epilogue

The world we live in is filled with confusing and sometimes contradictory demands, and it's very easy to forget that the most precious thing you have to fight for, at college and beyond, is your own integrity. Writing a good paper is part of that fight. It requires considerable courage, because there are so many forces conspiring to convince you that it's best for your success in the world to simply "follow the instructions." Sometimes those instructions, which may seem rational and useful, are so ill-considered that if you follow them passively you will have to put your capacity to think on hold. You can only do that for a very limited time before you become a patsy.

One of my implicit contentions in this book is that when you put off writing your essays for as long as possible you are probably doing so for a very good reason: so far, like the early Lance, you've found the task very unrewarding. This is the odd thing: although you don't find your thoughts in themselves uninteresting, they often sound flat and lifeless when you write them down. I've tried to encourage you to go beyond this valley of dead bones by thinking about the purpose and structure of your essays in a new way. It requires courage and a little practice but it's essentially grounded in common sense and, once you've shaken off the dead hand of the past, it will seem a much more straightforward and sensible way of expressing your ideas.

I need to say a word here in response to some important points raised by my students and colleagues. The first is something I touched on earlier but it needs revisiting. Many people have claimed that the hourglass model of exposition is very useful for those students who have no idea how to *begin* organizing their ideas into a whole. As I've argued, in certain circumstances this may be true, especially where you have a simple thesis which can be conveniently supported by three main arguments. For most essays this approach suffers from a number of disadvantages. Its formula does not allow you to be genuinely curious in the way that, for example, Vinnie or Rick or Jackson are in their respective essays. That's a very grave shortcoming because that's the main reason you came to college: to ask questions. While there are some problems and topics that allow for a clear resolution, others, as you well know, won't yield an easy answer, and certainly not an answer in three neat parts. Should we then exclude such questions from our essays? Of course not—they are the engines that drive us to think and write.

I have tried to demonstrate that the flaw in the hourglass model is deep in its DNA. Nothing very interesting can develop from it. In asserting that, my aim is not to make your life difficult but to point to something much more natural, and more liberating. Each essay you write using this new approach will be its own "narrative of ideas" and it will take its shape from those ideas. It will resist being crammed into a fixed formula.

At this point I need to offer a word of caution. As I mentioned in the introduction, you may, at certain times in your career, be under the instruction of someone who insists that you strictly follow a received form. As individual circumstances vary widely I can't offer any general advice on how to deal with this. You will have to rely on your own common sense. Many academic publications also insist on a specific way of organizing research papers and some teachers follow them rigidly and require their students to do so as well. Again, you'll have to make up your own mind how to act when such requirements are made of you. When, in order to survive, you do have to conform to a fixed mode of writing, having read this book, you will be aware that there are other possibilities you can use when the occasion suits.

When you begin to write in the way I've proposed throughout this book you will experience a sense of liberation and of pleasure. You will come to see that writing an essay resembles all honest work. Like an artist, the writer of a good essay has to concentrate on details, to find the exact word, to listen to the rhythm of his or her prose and to care about the overall elegance and purpose of the design. In doing so you will be freed from the old mold into a new kind of thinking, and it will never leave you.

As your skills deepen with this new way of thinking and writing you will almost certainly be opposed by people who, for their own reasons, will try to dissuade you. They will argue that it's safer (for them and for you) to stay within the old confines because, among other things, that will stop you asking awkward questions. They will be right. It's safer. But by now you know something better: as a great educator once said, education is very often a subversive activity. In other words, without awkward questions it's not possible to have an education worth a damn.

If you don't know that by now I haven't told you a very good story.

Acknowledgements

To Mark Heiman, friend and partner at Black Willow Press, my warmest thanks for seeing this book through all its stages, as well as for considerable help in the design and composition of the new edition. His remarkable eye and ear have, time and again, helped me break through some very stubborn difficulties. A number of colleagues and friends, at Carleton College and elsewhere, have given generous encouragement throughout the writing of this book and I want to thank, in particular, Roy Eleveton, Elizabeth Coville, James Fisher, Richard Crouter, Ann Patrick, Sigrun Leonard, Elie Noujain, Robert Tisdale, James McDonnell, Robert Bonner, Wayne Carver, Aurelia Armstrong, Andrea Witcombe, and Jenny Gibson, for her judicious criticism and proofreading.

Liz Ciner, who has accompanied me in this project from the very beginning, made numerous helpful suggestions at every turn, and without them this book would have been much the poorer. Professor Deborah Appleman, Chair of the Education Department at Carleton College, used the first edition of this book with her students in her Summer Writing Program in 2010. In the Fall of 2010 and 2011, Professor Kirsten Jamsen, Director of the Writing Program at the University of Minnesota, gave the ms. of this new edition critical trials with the students in her Writing Seminar. To both these colleagues and their students I owe special thanks for their valuable comments.

To Christina Harrison, and our daughters, Katrina and Rebecca, I owe triple debt. Not only have they read the book and proof-read in various drafts, they have made very constructive suggestions throughout and they have encouraged me at those times, known to all writers, when inspiration was flagging.

My long-term debt is to my students—at Carleton College and several other institutions—for not only discussing their problems with me in some depth but, in many cases, pointing to their solutions. I must emphasize, though, in spite of all the help I've received from these numerous sources, the views expressed in these pages are my sole responsibility.

Minneapolis, 2012

As a writer, translator and teacher of writing and literature, Keith Harrison has worked in Australia, where he was born, as well as in England, Canada and the United States. Known mainly as a poet, he has also written essays and plays and worked extensively in translation from French, German and Middle English. In London, where he published his first  two collections, he was Tutor in English at the University of London. For most of his subsequent professional career in North America he was Professor of English and Writer-in-Residence at Carleton College in Northfield, Minnesota, where he was also Editor-in-Chief of *The Carleton Miscellany*.

At Carleton he was one of the foundational members of the Environmental Studies Program, where one of his interests was the problem of turning scientific findings into readable prose. He has also had a continuing interest in the relation between the sciences and the humanities and the finding of a common ground between apparently disparate disciplines.

Harrison's poems and translations and essays have appeared in many magazines throughout the English-speaking world and his work has been represented in a dozen or so national anthologies in Australia, England and America. In 1998 his translation of *Sir Gawain and the Green Knight*, first published by the Folio Society of Great Britain, was selected for inclusion in the Oxford World's Classics Series. His collected poems, representing forty years' work, were published under the title of *Changes* in both Minneapolis and Melbourne in 2003. At present he is working on several books, including one for young poets on the crafts of poetry called *Word-Music*.

www.ingramcontent.com/pod-product-compliance
Lightning Source LLC
Chambersburg PA
CBHW060201050426
42446CB00013B/2929